MW01446260

GUIDED PRAYER JOURNAL

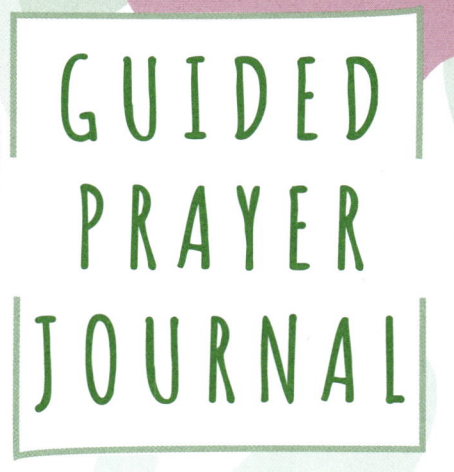

MISSIE BRANCH

B&H
PUBLISHING GROUP
Brentwood, Tennessee

To the many young ladies who have bravely shared their hearts with me. From my faves in the south who let me in and helped me grow, to those up north who trusted me with the vault. To the sisters who stayed after a conference, service, or class, and the three who call me Mom. Thank you! This is for you and because of you.

Text Copyright © 2024 by Missie Branch
All rights reserved.
Published by B&H Publishing Group, Brentwood, Tennessee
978-1-4300-9350-3
Dewey Decimal Classification: 248.3
Subject Heading: GIRLS / PRAYERS / DEVOTIONAL LITERATURE

Unless otherwise noted, Scripture quotations are taken from the Christian Standard Bible®, Copyright © 2017 by Holman Bible Publishers. Used by permission. Christian Standard Bible® and CSB® are federally registered trademarks of Holman Bible Publishers. Scripture quotations marked NIV are taken from the New International Version®, NIV® Copyright ©1973, 1978, 1984, 2011 by Biblica, Inc.® Used by permission. All rights reserved worldwide.
Scripture quotations marked ESV are taken from the English Standard Version. ESV® Text Edition: 2016. Copyright © 2001 by Crossway Bibles, a publishing ministry of Good News Publishers.
Scripture quotations marked NLT are taken from the New Living Translation, copyright © 1996, 2004, 2015 by Tyndale House Foundation. Used by permission of Tyndale House Publishers, Inc., Carol Stream, Illinois 60188. All rights reserved.
Scripture quotations marked MSG are taken from The Message copyright © 1993, 2002, 2018 by Eugene H. Peterson.

Printed in China, November 2023
1 2 3 4 5 6 7 · 28 27 26 25 24

NOTE TO READERS

It has been my dream to write this for you. When I was about seven years old, I truly believed that the God who made the entire world was listening to my prayers. My relationship with Him changed, and I started a habit of prayer then. I want you to have the same experience. This journal is for your conversations with God. He is so excited to hear from you.

Each day you will start with God's words and then a few words from me. Then it's time for your words. I will give you a few prompts, and you will have the chance to write out your prayers to God. Feel free to write as little or as much as you would like. No matter what, He hears you. Every prayer ends with a statement from my favorite hymn: "It is well." One line in the song says, "Whatever my lot, Thou hast taught me to say, It is well, it is well, with my soul." Those words have given me the courage to pray in hard times and the desire to pray in happy times. They have even helped restart my prayer journey in times I've fallen off.

The biblical king David wrote a prayer in Psalm 25. Part of it says, "Make your ways known to me, Lord; teach me your paths. Guide me in your truth and teach me, for you are the God of my salvation; I wait for you all day long." Today that is my prayer. I want it to become yours too. Learning to trust God with your thoughts may sound scary, but He is so good, and it is one of the best decisions you will ever make. I am so excited for you to be on this prayer journey with Jesus!

I'm praying for you,

Missie

1

You are saved by grace! He also raised us up with him and seated us with him in the heavens in Christ Jesus, so that in the coming ages he might display the immeasurable riches of his grace through his kindness to us in Christ Jesus. For you are saved by grace through faith, and this is not from yourselves; it is God's gift—not from works, so that no one can boast.
—Ephesians 2:5–9

I used to wonder why God made me. I would ask Him all the time. One day I read today's verses and I started to understand. We have been chosen, given His Spirit, gifted, loved on, and spared from spiritual death. God did all of it to allow others to see His kindness toward us. Grace is the Lord showering us with what we do not and could not deserve. God gave you life when you were born, and then He did it again and gave you spiritual life at your new birth in Christ!

God made you the way He did for you to be on display for Him. He intentionally chose your personality, ethnicity, height, and all your other wonderful details. It is all by His design. And He put you in your family, living in your community, at this time so that He could show the endless treasures of His grace. The Lord has saved you and is using you to bring Him glory. Who God made you to be is intentional. Why God has made you is to be a beautiful presentation of Him to the world.

Lord,

Thank You for showering me with Your grace. You made me intentionally and gifted me with . . .

_____

_____

_____

I have not always shown You great appreciation. Please help me not to take You for granted. Forgive me for not loving the way You made me when I . . .

_____

_____

_____

Being a walking display of Your goodness is a gift to me and those around me. Today, to point them to You, I want to focus on . . .

_____

_____

_____

_____

It is well. Amen.

2

For we are his workmanship, created in Christ Jesus for good works, which God prepared ahead of time for us to do.
—Ephesians 2:10

Some people can trace who they are related to for generations. I have always been told I look just like my dad. You may have the family nose or a grandparent's laugh or a unique personality quirk that shows everyone else who has influenced you. What you may not have considered is that no matter what your family looks like, you have been shaped by God. You are His handiwork, created skillfully and thoughtfully.

What is also true is that you have been created in Jesus to do good work for Him. This work is your purpose. Everyone's purpose should first show off how good God is to the world, and then it should change the lives of those around you. If you are a Christian, the Lord wants everyone to know you are His! You now have the Holy Spirit within you to help you do the work God has prepared for you.

Lord,

Thank You for creating me with a purpose. As I think about the work You have given me to do, I feel . . .

What I have learned about You is that . . .

Forgive me for not showing You off in parts of my life like . . .

Today I will show off Your goodness by . . .

It is well. Amen.

3

And you were dead in your trespasses and sins in which you previously walked according to the ways of this world, according to the ruler of the power of the air, the spirit now working in the disobedient. We too all previously lived among them in our fleshly desires, carrying out the inclinations of our flesh and thoughts, and we were by nature children under wrath as the others were also.
—Ephesians 2:1–3

Today's verses say that "you were dead in your trespasses and sins." Although it sounds like Paul is describing the latest zombie movie, he is not talking about physical death. Before anyone becomes a Christian, they are *spiritually* dead and living disconnected from Jesus Christ. When someone is walking "according to the ways of this world," it affects how they live—their daily habits, decisions, and relationships.

These verses make it clear that when we are spiritually dead, we are not just coasting through life in neutral. We are living as enemies of God. Before you become a Christian, your immoral desires and thoughts lead how you live. As a Christian, you have a new identity; you are different from before. You are no longer able to go on living like the people Paul calls "the disobedient." Now that you are alive spiritually, you can spend your days looking for ways to be more like Christ.

Lord,

Thank You for rescuing me from spiritual death. As I face today's challenges and victories, I am asking You to help me to . . .

_____
_____
_____

I do not want to live like the disobedient. Please forgive me for when I have. I confess that I . . .

_____
_____
_____
_____

As I live in You, I pray for the courage to . . .

_____
_____
_____
_____

so that I can look more like You.

It is well. Amen.

But God, who is rich in mercy, because of his great love that he had for us, made us alive with Christ even though we were dead in trespasses.
—Ephesians 2:4-5

All of us have a list of "I used to's" from another part of our lives. Things like "I used to suck my thumb," "I used to lie to my mom," or "I used to want to eat only fish crackers." But now, some of your "used to's" are behind you. You have grown a little, learned a few life lessons, and hopefully come to enjoy a wider variety of snacks.

In the same way, you should have a spiritual list of "I used to's." When you first became a Christian, you may have lied a lot or disrespected your parents. Looking back, you may see how silly or damaging your old behaviors were. Here's the blessing: that's who you *used* to be. God has transformed your spiritually dead self because of His huge love for you, and now you are alive in Christ. Who you were is not who you are anymore.

Lord,

Thank You for Your unending love for me. The reality of Your love encourages me to . . .

_____
_____
_____
_____

When I remember some of my "used to's," I want to ask You to forgive me for . . .

_____
_____
_____
_____

I am grateful to be maturing. I have learned that . . .

_____
_____
_____
_____

As I look forward to who I am becoming in Christ, today I commit to . . .

_____
_____
_____
_____

It is well. Amen.

5

Now if any of you lacks wisdom, he should ask God—who gives to all generously and ungrudgingly—and it will be given to him.
—James 1:5

I once heard a saying I have repeated to myself many times. I even put it up on the wall in my living room so that my family and friends can benefit from it too. It says, "Fools never learn. Smart people learn from their own mistakes. But wise people learn from the mistakes of others." These three simple truths can help carry a person through life. Making mistakes is inevitable, but if you can learn from them, they don't have to defeat or define you.

As a matter of fact, past failures can actually become keys to your growth. Learning and growing from mistakes is a sign of maturity. If you are wise, other people's mistakes will remind you to look for what God is teaching you. Instead of being like the fool in Proverbs 18:2 who isn't interested in understanding, those who take advice find wisdom (13:10). James tells us we can ask God for wisdom, and He gives generously.

Lord,

Thank You for not holding even the worst things I have done against me. I am asking You to forgive me for . . .

The Bible says the way to become wise is to learn from You. As I confess my mistake, what I have learned about it from You is . . .

What I can learn about myself is . . .

What I have learned about You through my mistake is . . .

It is well. Amen.

6

Set your minds on things above, not on earthly things. For you died, and your life is hidden with Christ in God.
—Colossians 3:2–3

The word *self-esteem* is used to describe a person's feelings about her own worth or value. In other words, how much you like and appreciate *you*. Self-esteem includes what you believe about your appearance, your emotions, and your behaviors. Processing who you are through the lens of who and what is or is not around you can be dangerous. Comparison becomes the measuring stick for judging your value.

A more helpful word is *self-image*. A positive self-image allows us to view ourselves the way God does—as beautiful, valuable, accepted, and necessary. After all, we were made in the *image* of God (Genesis 1:27). So what we feel about ourselves is not as important as what we know is true about Him. God has made humans at the top of all that He created, and He has made you to be like Him. Can you imagine it? The God of this entire universe made you intentionally, with a purpose, to have an impact. You don't have to esteem yourself; God already does.

Lord,

Thank You for reminding me that what You say is true. When it comes to self-esteem, I have seen myself as . . .

_____
_____
_____

What I have learned about You is . . .

_____
_____
_____

Help me to view myself the way You do! Please forgive me for every time I have not. I want to remember that You say I am . . .

_____
_____
_____
_____

Colossians says to put my mind on things above. Today I will focus my thoughts on . . .

_____
_____
_____

It is well. Amen.

7

How I love your instruction! It is my meditation all day long.
—Psalm 119:97

When I first became a Christian, I didn't understand how important it is to spend time reading the Bible, and I neglected it. Though I loved to read, I thought reading God's Word was boring. There was no way you could get me to understand why I needed to read old laws or a list of who was the dad of who in someone's family tree. But as I began to take time to study the Bible, I realized it was rewiring me. Why? Because as I read, I ran into God everywhere. And no one has an encounter with God and stays the same.

If you are truly in a relationship with God, who you were last year or even last month is different than who you are now. You can't experience God and not change. Now, you may still wonder what is even going on in the book of Revelation, and that's okay. If you prioritize a regular habit of spending time reading God's Word, one day you will realize that you've changed. You'll never be the same.

Lord,

Thank You for Your plan to make me more like You. When it comes to spending time reading the Bible, I feel ...

What this teaches me about myself is ...

I want to be like the psalmist who loves Your instruction. Please forgive me for the times I have neglected to ...

I want to be dedicated to connecting with You. Today I commit to ...

It is well. Amen.

Finally brothers and sisters, whatever is true, whatever is honorable, whatever is just, whatever is pure, whatever is lovely, whatever is commendable—if there is any moral excellence and if there is anything praiseworthy—dwell on these things.
—Philippians 4:8

I once heard a pastor say that we live in houses made of our thoughts. When I first pictured it, I envisioned a glass house with thought bubbles floating around. But a glass house is transparent and not hard to get in or out of. The more I thought about it, the "houses" where our thoughts live are usually more like prisons with high walls, metal doors, and barbed wire. Our thoughts are left trapped.

Your mind is an incredible information processor, but it is flawed because of sin. This flaw is the reason today's verse reminds you how to think. Your thoughts should not stay trapped, living as prisoners in your mind. It is your responsibility to make sure they are truthful and lifegiving. One way to do this is to share and process with other healthy Christians. Your thoughts should bring honor to the Lord because He is God, and to yourself because you are precious.

Lord,

Thank You for reminding me to think like You. When it comes to my thoughts, I have probably focused too much on . . .

Help me to let my mind be shaped by Yours. Please forgive me for any unhealthy, dishonoring thoughts. I want to remember to think about things that are . . .

Philippians encourages me to be an intentional thinker. Today I will focus my thoughts on . . .

It is well. Amen.

9

Listen to counsel and receive instruction so that you may be wise later in life. Many plans are in a person's heart, but the Lord's decree will prevail.
—Proverbs 19:20–21

I remember the sad day that changed my future. After applying, waiting, and celebrating that I had been accepted to the college of my dreams, I found out I would not be going. I realized then that God has different plans for me than the ones I have for myself. I needed to learn to trust Him with my life and to be patient with His vision for me. It was hard to do, and I was not very happy about it. But my mom kept reminding me that the Lord's plan for us is always good.

At some point in your life, God will interrupt your agenda with His own. You may not end up with the life you hoped for, and it can feel like God is withholding happiness from you. He is not. Trust Him. It's possible to learn to want His plan for you. You may even see His dreams for you become your own. Mom was right—God's plan for your life is always good, and it will succeed.

LORD,

Thank You for caring about me and for having a design for my life. When I think about trusting You with my life, I feel . . .

Help me to be hopeful about my future. Please forgive me for when I have doubted Your plan. I want to remember that You are good even when . . .

You are wise, and Your plans will always work out for my good. Today I commit to trust You with my plans for . . .

IT IS WELL. AMEN.

10

For it was you who created my inward parts; you knit me together in my mother's womb. I will praise you because I have been remarkably and wondrously made. Your works are wondrous, and I know this very well.
—Psalm 139:13-14

Everybody wants to be known for something. I definitely do. The mistake I made was trying to create things to be known for. I wanted people to think of me as a musician, an athlete, and a super smart student because I wanted to be needed and seen as important. That was my entire motivation—not the love of the thing, but the love of being recognized for it.

This way of thinking ties your value to someone else's feelings. It means you are only as important as "they" think you are. This is not God's idea. Who you are is not defined by your looks, talents, relationship status, education, who your parents are, or the affirmation that you (and I) may desire from friends. God made you wonderfully, and He loves you. He has given you value. You are already important, and you have been made extraordinary by Him.

Lord,

Thank You for knowing me fully and loving me deeply. When I think about who You made me to be, I feel . . .

_____
_____
_____
_____

Help me to look to You for my value and worth. Please forgive me for when I have looked for it in . . .

_____
_____
_____
_____

Today's verses remind me that I am Your work and that Your work is wonderful. I am important because I have been made by You! Today I choose to be grateful that You specifically made me to be . . .

_____
_____
_____

It is well. Amen.

LORD, here's who and what I'm praying for . . .

I'm grateful You've answered these prayers . . .

11

Therefore, if anyone is in Christ, he is a new creation; the old has passed away, and see, the new has come!
—2 Corinthians 5:17

You live in a time when everyone is searching for identity differently than earlier generations did. Back then, people may have dealt with confusing who they *are* with what they *do*, but today it also matters how many people *know* you for it. But the Lord didn't make you to be just another cute face online. Who you are is so much more.

The center of what it means to be a Christian is that we have been given a new identity. You have been upgraded to reflect all that Jesus Christ is. The things you do in your life have value, but your identity is directly tied to the work Christ has already done. So who are you? You are not the total of your likes, your followers, or your friends. You are so much more.

Lord,

Thank You for rescuing me from who I used to be and making me new in You. When I think about how my life would be without knowing You, I am grateful that...

Help me to find my identity fully in You. Please forgive me for trying to find myself in...

Today as I focus on being made new in You, I will reflect You to those around me by...

It is well. Amen.

12

"Remain in me, and I in you. Just as a branch is unable to produce fruit by itself unless it remains on the vine, neither can you unless you remain in me."
—John 15:4

I love to read. Occasionally as I'm reading, I need to pause to find out what a word means. When the word has more than one definition, I have to figure out what it means to the author. In today's verse I think it makes sense to find out what it means to *remain*. I did some research and found that to *remain* is to be steady or stable. It also means to rest. It is both an invitation and a command.

Just like little kids who fight against going to sleep at naptime, we often push against the stability and rest God has provided for us. Could it be that, like little kids, we haven't grasped how good rest and stability can be for us? How about you? If you are honest with yourself, have you taken for granted or even misunderstood the command to remain in Christ? Have you ignored the invitation to have peace of mind in Him? If so, today is the perfect day to start accepting Jesus's invitation. He is inviting you to exhale and to enjoy the stability and rest you can have in your relationship with Him.

Lord,

Thank You for providing me with both stability and rest. As I grow my relationship with You, I know I can experience rest by . . .

Today's verse teaches that beautiful fruit is produced when I remain in You. Please forgive me for foolishly trying to do these things without You . . .

To grow more stable in my faith, I need to stay close to You. That means I should prioritize my relationship with You. Today I will be intentional to . . .

It is well. Amen.

13

*L̶ord̶, who can dwell in your tent? Who can live on your holy mountain? The one who lives blamelessly, practices righteousness, and acknowledges the truth in his heart—who does not slander with his tongue, **who does not harm his friend, or discredit his neighbor** . . .—the one who does these things will never be shaken.*
—Psalm 15:1-3, 5

Have you ever been robbed? I have! For a while my family lived in Philadelphia, and I can't count how many bikes we had stolen. The saddest time was when four bikes were taken from our house at once! The fear of being robbed again lingered long after we moved away. Even if your things are returned, a robbery can leave you feeling afraid, suspicious, anxious, and vulnerable.

You may have never stolen someone's bike, but you may have unknowingly made someone feel robbed. Today's psalm points out the person who does not discredit their neighbor. An easy way to discredit other people is through gossip. Gossiping is a lot like robbing someone. It takes their stories, issues, words, or information without their permission and uses them like they're yours. And it leaves people feeling victimized. Today's verses describe the opposite of gossipers. They tell of those who have truly experienced God. God is a good Father who protects fiercely, and people who spend their days with Him will learn to avoid gossip and instead behave like Him.

LORD,

Thank You for the Bible showing me how to be more like You. I understand how hurtful gossip can be. What I have learned about You is . . .

I want to be more like You. Help me to guard my tongue. Please forgive me for when I have gossiped about . . .

Gossiping affects Your reputation and mine. Today if I am tempted to gossip, instead I will . . .

IT IS WELL. AMEN.

14

*Lord, who can dwell in your tent? Who can live on your holy mountain? The one who lives blamelessly, practices righteousness, and acknowledges the truth in his heart . . . **who despises the one rejected by the Lord** but honors those who fear the Lord . . . the one who does these things will never be shaken.*
—Psalm 15:1-2, 4-5

This psalm describes those who have truly experienced God. It says they despise "the one rejected by the Lord." But who is that? Satan. God's evil, arrogant, and wicked enemy. When I hear the word *wicked*, I imagine fictional movie characters who are often old, mean, and overpowered in the end. But because of Satan, truly wicked people do exist. In the Bible we read about Haman, Esther's enemy, and Ahab, who God said was the most wicked king Israel ever had.

In contrast, who are those "who fear the Lord"? These are godly people, meaning they live lives that are committed to Jesus and His authority. The Bible is full of real-life examples of godly people. Daniel, Ruth, Esther, Josiah, Joshua, and Mary were determined to honor the Lord with their lives. All of them made this commitment at a young age! When we follow these godly examples and despise the wicked, we show God that we believe in Him and His truth.

Lord,

Thank You for the Bible's examples of people who were committed to You. Your great love makes people want to be godly. I would like to grow to be more like . . .

because that person . . .

I want to love what You love, Lord. Please forgive me for loving things You don't love, such as . . .

Help me to know what a godly life looks like at my age. I commit to growing in godliness today by . . .

It is well. Amen.

15

*Lord, who can dwell in your tent? Who can live on your holy mountain? The one who lives blamelessly, practices righteousness, and acknowledges the truth in his heart . . . **who keeps his word whatever the cost** . . . the one who does these things will never be shaken.*
—Psalm 15:1-2, 4-5

We all know that person known for not keeping her word. If I were to be honest, it used to be me. I couldn't see how much trust I broke every time I didn't follow through on my promises. Sadly, it impacted the way people saw my Christianity. This psalm describes people who have truly experienced God. They keep their word even if it costs them something big. Doing what you said you would do is a way to exercise your faith.

Every day you have the chance to be true to your words. Will you be there at 8 p.m. like you said, or will you run a little behind while finishing up that last episode? Will you still give money to a friend who needs it when you realize you'll be broke if you do? Will you show up and volunteer at church now that you've been invited somewhere fun? People who spend time with God keep their word, even when it hurts. We do this because the choices we make daily reflect what we truly believe.

Lord,

Thank You for allowing time spent with You to make me better. As I think about experiencing You more, I would like to spend time . . .

I want to keep my word. I ask You to remind me of this daily. Please forgive me for when I have not honored commitments. I will be more careful to . . .

What I have learned about myself today is . . .

Today as I focus on being trustworthy, I will remember to . . .

It is well. Amen.

16

Whatever you do, do it from the heart, as something done for the Lord and not for people, knowing that you will receive the reward of an inheritance from the Lord. You serve the Lord Christ.
—Colossians 3:23-24

I remember when I could not wait to get my first job. I thought that working would be the ultimate freedom. I would have my own money to spend however I wanted. But when I received my first paycheck, I found out a job wasn't the fantasy I thought it was going to be. My mom expected me to pay for my uniforms and transportation and to help pay for things in our home. Once reality set in, I was not excited to work anymore.

Back then, I needed a better understanding of God's plan for our work. Because of the effects of sin, work can be hard and exhausting. That is why God has also given us the gift of rest. But we must be careful not to separate work and rest in our minds in a way that makes work bad and rest good. Whether it's schoolwork or a job or helping others at home or church, your work is good. It should be done with all your heart. Everyone must do some type of work, and when you do it for God, He will reward your effort to serve Him well.

Lord,

Thank You for giving me the gift of work. As I think about serving You with the rest of my life, I feel . . .

All my jobs, ministry opportunities, and service to others are a part of the work You have given me to do. Help me not to look down on any of it. Please forgive me for when I have been ungrateful for . . .

Today as I do the work You have given me to do, I commit to . . .

It is well. Amen.

17

Then Jesus said to his disciples, "If anyone wants to follow after me, let him deny himself, take up his cross, and follow me. For whoever wants to save his life will lose it, but whoever loses his life because of me will find it."
—MATTHEW 16:24-25

My mom was a single mother. She worked two jobs and still made sure my sister and I were in church and involved in every school activity. Mom did a lot of denying herself to provide for us. Whenever I think of living sacrificially, I think of her. Maybe you've seen your parents give up their own needs to provide for you and your family. But today's verse is talking about a different kind of sacrifice: denying ourselves so that we can give our lives to God.

One of the hardest things to do is to deny yourself completely. Some girls avoid junk food to fit in smaller jeans, or they work extra hours to go on a trip with friends. But you can't equate those types of personal "sacrifices" to the kind of losing Jesus describes in Matthew 16. He asks you to change your motives, embrace humility, and reject a lifestyle that revolves around yourself. Jesus denied Himself in those ways for you. Taking up your cross means daily staying loyal to Christ and your faith in Him. He promises that if you do, you will find new life in the process.

Lord,

Thank You for being a God who models the goodness You are looking for in me. As I think about what it means to lose my life to find a new one in You, I feel . . .

What I am learning about You is . . .

I know that You care for me and want me to flourish, but learning to deny myself isn't easy. Forgive me for when I have been selfish. I confess that I . . .

As I am learning to develop a healthy spiritual life and deny myself for You, today the one thing I will focus on is . . .

It is well. Amen.

18

*Therefore, brothers and sisters, make every effort
to confirm your calling and election, because if you
do these things you will never stumble.*
—2 Peter 1:10

Christians have their own language. We say things to each other that might seem really strange to some people. We like to use the words *call* and *calling* a lot. When I was younger, I thought a calling was a one-time, special telephone conversation everyone got to have with God to understand who they are. That would be nice! Although He doesn't pick up a phone and call us, God does give us opportunities to learn from Him about our lives.

A calling is the vocation or work God has created us to do. There are individual calls, and there are callings that everyone is responsible for. The Bible teaches that God calls all of us to behave like Jesus Christ and to take care of the earth. We should also be wise with our time, our gifts, and our money. God calls us to trust Him, to be in a real relationship with Him and each other, to serve each other, and to tell others about Him.

Lord,

Thank You for allowing me to join other Christians in serving You. As I look at the calling You have for us, I see that You want me to . . .

Doing those things will protect me. Please forgive me for not trusting Your goodness when I choose to . . .

Thinking about the calling You have for all Christians, today I will focus on . . .

It is well. Amen.

19

*His divine power has given us everything required
for life and godliness through the knowledge of him
who called us by his own glory and goodness.*
—2 Peter 1:3

When my son, Jay, was only four, I told him that God had chosen him to be the oldest. I made it clear that being the big brother comes with responsibility and that he was expected to be excellent. His three sisters may not have loved how seriously he took it, but even at four he had a God-given calling on his life. He did not have to wait until he was an adult to live it out.

What about you? Are you the oldest sibling? The middle? An only child? Have you ever looked at that as part of your calling? God did. He gave you unique talents as well. If you are an artist, a math pro, an athlete, or a natural encourager, God gave you that ability, and it is your responsibility to steward it well to bring Him glory.

The next several entries explore different kinds of callings, including an internal call, an external call, and formal call. Your calling is your purpose. It's the mission God has given you to do as a unique individual so that your life can point others to Him.

Lord,

Thank You for having a purpose for my life. You made all of me to bring You glory. What I have learned about the unique gifts and talents You have given me is . . .

It is amazing to me how concerned You are with Your people. Please forgive me for when I have not been willing to recognize Your love for me. When I feel insecure about it, I will . . .

I want to live with purpose. Help me to continue learning what Your plan is for me. Today I will live out my calling by . . .

It is well. Amen.

20

Now there are different gifts, but the same Spirit. There are different ministries, but the same Lord. And there are different activities, but the same God works all of them in each person.
—1 Corinthians 12:4–6

I love to watch singing competitions. My favorite parts are the auditions when someone obviously meant to be a star has no idea they can sing so well. I am moved by the judges' reactions and the sheer surprise the singer has when they see the response. But sometimes I am jealous. I have even been sad that God did not give me the ability to sing well enough to audition for a singing competition. But if I choose to actually be mad at God about my lack of certain skills, that would be sinful. God has been intentional with the gifts He has given me. I have to accept His "no" on the others.

As you try to figure out the plans God has said "yes" to for your life, it's good to recognize specific kinds of callings. One is an internal feeling that God made you to do something specific. It could be your desire to do some form of Christian work or what drives you to go to law school. God has crafted each of us with different sensitivities, motivations, and ways of thinking. That's why some people are passionate about politics and others, the planet. Your most important work can often be found by understanding the distinct way God has wired you.

Lord,

Thank You for making me unique. Thinking about what You would say "yes" to, I could imagine becoming a . . .

I understand that sin can cause me to question how You have made me. Please forgive me for the times when I have not appreciated . . .

To determine what You have made me for, I want to evaluate the natural gifts You've given me. Today I will be thankful for my ability to . . .

It is well. Amen.

LORD, here's who and what I'm praying for . . .

I'm grateful You've answered these prayers . . .

21

If the whole body were an eye, where would the hearing be? If the whole body were an ear, where would the sense of smell be? But as it is, God has arranged each one of the parts in the body just as he wanted. And if they were all the same part, where would the body be? As it is, there are many parts, but one body.
—1 Corinthians 12:17-20

I love to encourage my friends to join an art class, do a service project, or look for a particular opportunity at church. Why? Because I like to watch people thrive in their natural gifts and abilities. I probably should have been a school guidance counselor because I just really love seeing people do things they are good at.

You have been given gifts (for ministry and other good works) that you will succeed in naturally. This is your external call. Everyone's call is unique to them. Often the people who know you best can recognize and encourage that "something special" God has made in you. For this external call, it's wise to use humility and maturity and to rely on your Christian community. They can help you understand when and how to use your unique abilities in ways that show why God entrusted them to you.

Lord,

Thank You for giving me gifts to do Your good works. One gift that people have seen in me is . . .

___

___

You have designed every person to need another person. Community is a gift from You. Please forgive me for when I have not had the humility to . . .

___

___

___

What I am learning about myself is . . .

___

___

___

___

Growing in You and serving others are two ways my friends and family can recognize my external calling. Today I will explore my gifts by . . .

___

___

___

___

It is well. Amen.

22

Just as each one has received a gift, use it to serve others, as good stewards of the varied grace of God. If anyone speaks, let it be as one who speaks God's words; if anyone serves, let it be from the strength God provides, so that God may be glorified through Jesus Christ in everything. To him be the glory and the power forever and ever. Amen.
—1 Peter 4:10–11

Sometimes it's hard to imagine how God can use me. We all know that God uses the pastor, but what about those of us who are students or have regular jobs? What if I don't want to work at my church? You may not have been told this before, but that's okay. Yes, we need pastors and missionaries, but we also need Christians who are teachers, social workers, dentists, and students. Working in Christian ministry is wonderful, but it is not a higher calling; it is a different calling.

Another way to understand the work God has for you is known as a formal call, which could look like an opportunity to intern at an organization or a chance to go to a particular school that prepares you for the work He has for you. Pay attention to what in your life seems to confirm your giftedness and lines up with your internal and external calls. But no matter what you are doing, you are called to be a full-time Christian, working for Christ through all of it.

Lord,

Thank You for being able to use me where I am today. As I think of ways to serve You now, I would like to ask You about . . .

No matter what work I do, I want to be doing it for You. Please forgive me for when I . . .

As I think about the opportunities that may come my way, I want to be prepared to display You in all I do. Please help me to . . .

It is well. Amen.

23

So if you have been raised with Christ, seek the things above, where Christ is, seated at the right hand of God. Set your minds on things above, not on earthly things.
—Colossians 3:1-2

When I think about my childhood, things were hard for my family. But even when things were bad, I can remember going to church and seeing how happy Jesus made people. Watching them made me want to be happy too. The Lord used their example to lead me to Him, and I eventually became a Christian. What I didn't understand as a new believer was that everything about my identity had changed. I was no longer just a daughter or sister or the girl with the hard life; I had been given a new life in Christ. I needed to change the way I lived, talked, and more importantly, the way I thought.

If you're a Christian, your identity is in Christ. But this identity is not passive, like it was when you were born. God created you, your mother carried you, your parents named you, and now people celebrate you every year. You didn't do a thing! But to thrive in your new identity as a Christian will require effort, like choosing joy when things are hard. God wants you to be thinking about things that concern Him. This is what today's verse means when it says to "set your mind on things above." If you let it, your new identity in Christ will shift your focus and expand your thinking in amazing ways!

Lord,

Thank You for giving me a new identity. Each day I want to look more like You. As I think about shifting the way I think, I can see that it requires me to...

Seeking the things above means wanting the same things You want. Help me, Lord, to make that a reality in my life. Forgive me for when I instead want...

Today, as I set my mind on things above, I will focus on...

It is well. Amen.

24

Let us lay aside every hindrance and the sin that so easily ensnares us. Let us run with endurance the race that lies before us, keeping our eyes on Jesus, the pioneer and perfecter of our faith.
—Hebrews 12:1-2

If I put a lid on a jar with a lit candle in it, what will happen? The flame will go out. Why? Because it has no oxygen. If I cut off all light to my plants, they will die. Why? They were denied light. But denial is not always bad. If I deny my body huge amounts of sugar, I can become healthier. If I deny myself the sinful habits that I have created, I can become healthier spiritually.

The things in your life that trip you up and cause you to stumble in your faith need to be cut off, deprived of oxygen. You carry them like unnecessary weights, and they get in the way of God's plan for you. They often distort reality, cause confusion, and send you running to other people for affirmation instead of to Christ, who is your life. Jesus invites you to cut off your unhealthy habits and to journey through life with Him.

Lord,

Thank You for sacrificing Your life for mine. I want to live a spiritually healthy life. For me this can look like . . .

_____
_____
_____

I understand that everyone deals with sin in their lives. Please forgive me for when I have not immediately dealt with . . .

_____
_____
_____
_____

What I am learning about Your plan for my life is . . .

_____
_____
_____
_____

I want to get in the habit of denying myself old sinful habits. Today I commit to . . .

_____
_____
_____

It is well. Amen.

25

*Therefore, put to death what belongs to your
earthly nature: sexual immorality, impurity, lust,
evil desire, and greed, which is idolatry.*
—Colossians 3:5

Today's verse covers sins involving our bodies. Although the writer here was blunt, Christians are often uncomfortable talking about these kinds of struggles. Many of us wrestle with immorality, whether it's in a dating relationship or through inappropriate shows, music, or online conversations. We live in a society that is okay with all of it, so it can be hard to recognize these sins in our lives and even harder to understand why they are so dangerous.

If we were to trace most of our sin issues to their root, almost all of them would have started on this list. These sins are sneaky, can lead to destructive addictions, and all have the same source: idolatry. Idolatry happens when we look to people or things to make us happy. Too often, Christians turn to all kind of things that are offensive to God rather than looking to Him for what only He can give. God wants you to let go of the idols you may have in your life in exchange for His gifts—things like satisfaction, meaning, contentment, and peace.

Lord,

Thank You for exposing sin in my life. Being honest with You, Lord, is safe. As I read this verse, I see that You dislike . . .

Idolizing things and people is easy to do. Forgive me for when I have idolized . . .

Today I choose to pursue You. I will focus on . . .

It is well. Amen.

26

But now, put away all the following: anger, wrath, malice, slander, and filthy language from your mouth. Do not lie to one another, since you have put off the old self with its practices and have put on the new self. You are being renewed in knowledge according to the image of your Creator.
—Colossians 3:8–10

When I was younger, I decided that cursing was dumb and I wouldn't do it. In my mind, I had to remember a million different spelling words and their definitions for too many years to keep using the same four words for every one of my emotions. Although there is some truth there, my motivation did not represent the high call of my identity in Christ. And if I ever did curse, I felt like an imposter because deep down I knew that the Lord deserved better from me as His daughter.

Our identity as Christians requires us to be intentional and active. We have to learn to deny our old sinful selves by being in control of our emotions, our thoughts, our relationships, and our mouths. And we must remember that our motives matter. Today's verses remind us that we are being renewed—changed into the image of our Creator. The "you" that God is remaking is being changed from the inside out. We control our words and our behavior because we are His, and that is enough.

Lord,

Thank You for pushing me to live like I am being renewed in You. As I read the list in these verses, I am challenged to change the way I . . .

Putting off my old sinful ways is active, not passive. Forgive me for when I have been . . .

Today, as I choose to be active in putting on my new self, I will focus on . . .

It is well. Amen.

27

Therefore, as God's chosen ones, holy and dearly loved, put on compassion, kindness, humility, gentleness, and patience.
—Colossians 3:12

If you were a woman in Colossae when today's verse was first delivered, these words would have been so crazy to hear. The women of that time and place would not have thought of themselves as chosen. They spent most of their days doing housework. When these women did leave their homes, their value would be measured by the clothes they put on. So when the women heard that they were not seen by God as domestic workers but as His chosen ones who were to put on compassion and kindness for the world to see, it would have been so impactful for them. As followers of Christ, their identities had been upgraded, even if their lifestyles had not.

The writer, Paul, is asking you to invest in a new way of thinking, a new way of going through life. As you continue to deny oxygen to your old sinful habits, you should be investing in a new spiritual wardrobe. The clothes you wear to school or work or church or anywhere else make a statement about who you are, what you like, and what you believe. Spiritual clothes—compassion, humility, gentleness, and patience—show the same things. What does your spiritual wardrobe say about you?

Lord,

Thank You for choosing me. When I read that I am holy and dearly loved by You, I feel . . .

Changing my spiritual wardrobe has to be intentional. Forgive me for when I instead choose to wear . . .

I am learning that I am . . .

As I think about today's verse, I will focus on . . .

It is well. Amen.

28

Therefore, as God's chosen ones, holy and dearly loved, put on compassion, kindness, humility, gentleness, and patience, bearing with one another and forgiving one another if anyone has a grievance against another. Just as the Lord has forgiven you, so you are also to forgive.
—Colossians 3:12-13

A while ago, I experienced a hurt I didn't think I would recover from. In the middle of the pain, no one could convince me that forgiveness was possible. Things were already tough, and I didn't want to think about adding another hard thing. As I began to heal, Christians in my life reminded me of the words found here in Colossians. They challenged me to do what the Lord had done for me: to forgive.

When people refuse to forgive, it's often because they don't remember how many times they have been forgiven. The act of forgiving is both a decision in your mind and a journey of your heart, and God requires it of us. Forgiving others does not mean the pain didn't happen, and it doesn't free the other person of consequences. What it does is free you from the weight of the grudges you carry, and it reminds you that you are not God. He judges perfectly; we don't. My road to forgiveness was long and hard, but I did ultimately obey. I stopped clinging to my old decaying heart and chose to rely on the new life and strength provided for me in Christ. And now I am free.

Lord,

I am not perfect. Thank You for forgiving me. I know it cost You a lot. When I think about forgiving someone who has hurt me, I feel . . .

Forgiving people when they hurt me is difficult to do. Forgive me for when I chose not to forgive someone for . . .

Because I am forgiven, today I will . . .

It is well. Amen.

29

And let the peace of Christ . . . rule your hearts. . . . Let the word of Christ dwell richly among you, in all wisdom teaching and admonishing one another . . . with gratitude in your hearts. And whatever you do, in word or in deed, do everything in the name of the Lord Jesus, giving thanks to God the Father through him.
—Colossians 3:15–17

When my kids were younger, they memorized Bible verses related to the letters of the alphabet. When they would fight, I would make them recite the letter "s": "Seek peace and pursue it" (Psalm 34:14). I made pursing peace their responsibility, just like it is mine. Today's verses are similar to that psalm. They give us instructions for how to navigate our identity in Christ. Not just to make us better, but for those in Christ around us. The Lord has established peace, and now we get to manage it. His peace is our gift.

The women in this Colossae community were being given more responsibility. They were told to pursue Christ's peace, to teach and challenge each other, to live with gratitude, and to do all of it in the name of Jesus, remembering to thank God. This kind of expectation for women was radical, because in their new lives as followers of Christ, their true value was being revealed. Their lives were no longer just about getting through life, and neither is yours. God is giving you permission to experience His peace, to live fully and breathe deeply in Him.

Lord,

Thank You for providing me a pathway to peace. When I think about how this can change my life, I feel . . .

_____
_____
_____

What I have learned about You today is . . .

_____
_____
_____

I am often my biggest barrier to the good You have for me. Please forgive me for when I have not prioritized . . .

_____
_____
_____

These verses remind me that Your peace is a gift. Today I will seek peace and pursue it by . . .

_____
_____
_____

It is well. Amen.

30

The one who lives under the protection of the Most High dwells in the shadow of the Almighty.
—Psalm 91:1

I grew up without my dad. I knew he loved me, but there were times I felt vulnerable because he was not around to protect me. Today's verse begins one of my favorite chapters in the Bible. I have turned to it over and over again when I've felt afraid. The phrase "shadow of the Almighty" makes me think of a comforting hiding place, a bit like when I hid in my mom's closet as a girl while playing hide-and-seek with my cousins. Maybe you can imagine being under a warm, cozy blanket on a cold day. It's a feeling of safety, the one you have when you are with the people you love.

The shadow in today's verse actually points to the protection that comes from being hidden in Jesus. This protection is not just for the fatherless who feel vulnerable. It is for all believers who have put their trust in Christ. Hebrews 13:5 says, "He himself has said, 'I will never leave you or abandon you.'" For those of us who live with our fears and weakness close to the surface, the truth of God's commitment and protection can calm our anxieties and provide His much-needed peace.

Lord,

Thank You for being my protector and inviting me to find safety in You. Based on my experience with fear, this truth makes me feel . . .

_____
_____
_____
_____

This verse is a reminder for those who trust in You. Please forgive me for when I do not trust You to . . .

_____
_____
_____
_____

Today I will show my commitment to You by . . .

_____
_____
_____
_____

It is well. Amen.

LORD, here's who and what I'm praying for . . .

I'm grateful You've answered these prayers . . .

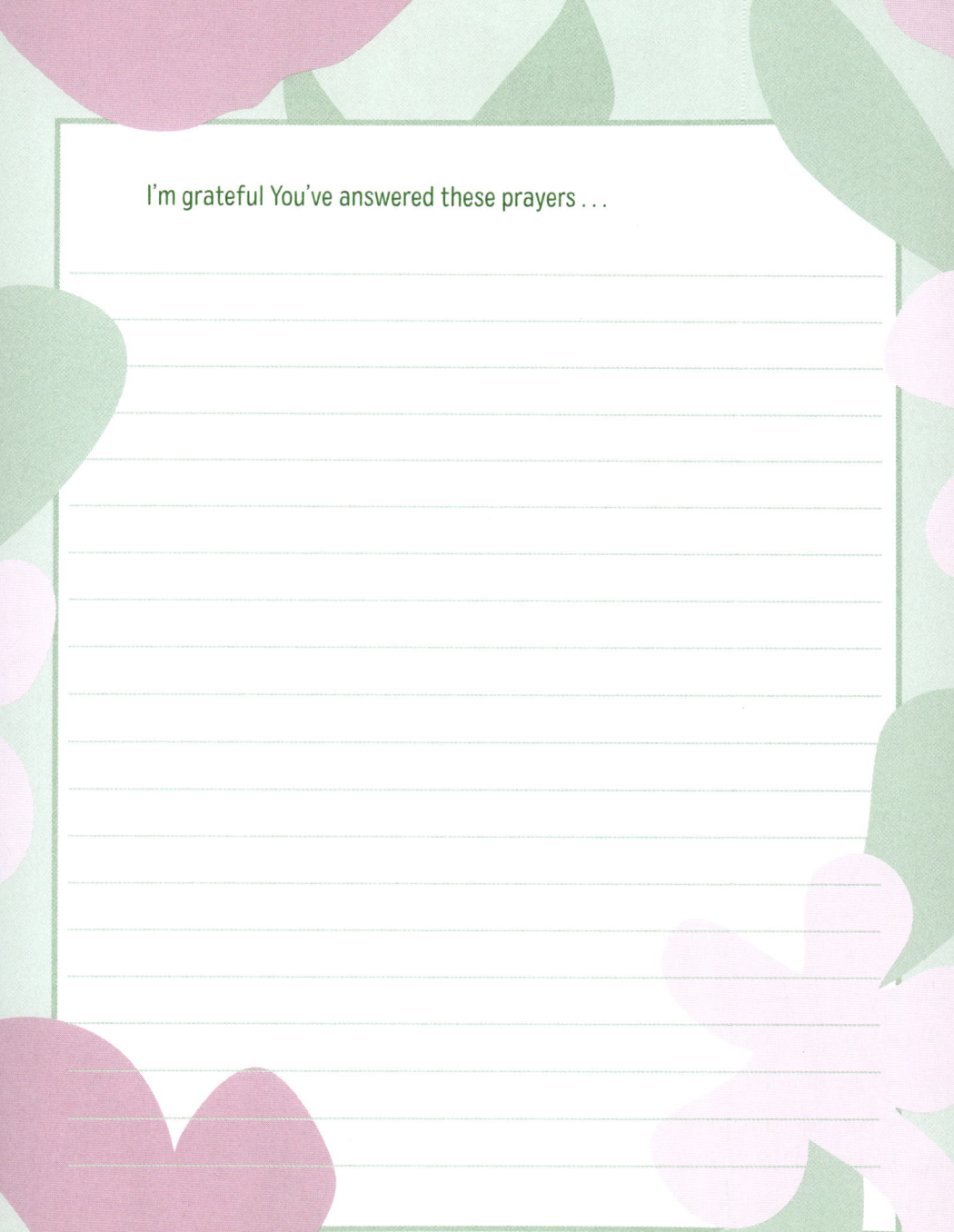

31

"So whenever you give to the poor, don't sound a trumpet before you, as the hypocrites do in the synagogues and on the streets, to be applauded by people. Truly I tell you, they have their reward. But when you give to the poor, don't let your left hand know what your right hand is doing, so that your giving may be in secret. And your Father who sees in secret will reward you."
—Matthew 6:2-4

I read a book called *The Jesus Habits* that lists thirty-one habits Jesus was committed to, habits for us to imitate today. One of those was giving. Jesus gave His time, His body, His rights, His wealth, and His life. He did acts of service as He healed the sick and the lame, raised the dead, and fed the hungry. And then He almost always told these people not to tell anyone about what He had done for them. Why? One reason is He didn't want the focus to be just the giving or the miracles. Jesus didn't want the blind people to just see; He wanted them to see Him as their Savior.

Jesus gave sacrificially, with a full understanding of His purpose—to bring worship to God the Father. He expected His disciples to do the same thing. His goal for you is to give. But when you do, be sure of your motivation. Make sure it is not for attention, likes, or to impress a guy. Every time you give, imagine it being placed directly into Jesus's hands. God sees your giving and will reward you.

Lord,

Thank You for not just telling me to give but for modeling it. Your example encourages me to . . .

_____
_____
_____
_____

Giving with the right motivation upgrades our giving experiences. Please forgive me for when my heart has been distracted by . . .

_____
_____
_____
_____

Today I am motivated to give . . .

_____
_____
_____
_____

It is well. Amen.

32

"But when you pray, go into your private room, shut your door, and pray to your Father who is in secret. And your Father who sees in secret will reward you."
—Matthew 6:6

I recently read a book where the author imagined Jesus singing. I have never thought about it, but it makes sense. Jesus went to services in the temple, He went to school, and He walked for miles (which meant lots of time for singing). It's beautiful to think that He may have sung with His disciples. We know He taught them how to worship, and in today's verse He was teaching them how to pray. Jesus definitely modeled a life filled with prayer. Luke 5:16 tells us that He frequently went away to the wilderness to pray. Sometimes He would pray all night.

Jesus prayed for all His followers, and He prayed prayers of sadness and prayers of thanksgiving. But when Jesus taught the disciples how to pray in Matthew 6:6, He told them to go and pray privately. Edwin Keith once said, "Prayer is exhaling the spirit of man and inhaling the spirit of God." This time alone with Jesus is for your benefit, not His. So pray regularly and about anything. But when you pray, don't do it because you think you have to. Remember your Father is always listening.

Lord,

Thank You for not just telling me to pray but for modeling it. Your example encourages me to . . .

_____
_____
_____
_____
_____
_____

A Christian who does not pray is not spiritually healthy. Please forgive me for when I have treated prayer like . . .

_____
_____
_____
_____
_____
_____

Today I am motivated to pray for . . .

_____
_____
_____
_____

It is well. Amen.

33

Do not take the Lord's discipline lightly or lose heart when you are reproved by him, for the Lord disciplines the one he loves.
—Hebrews 12:5-6

As a kid, my choices and my mom's standards collided enough times for me to understand the idea of consequences. I remember a day when I saw a boy yelling at his mom at the grocery store. I couldn't help but worry about him. As I watched this scene, my mom bent down to my ear and whispered calmly, "If you even think about it, you will be grounded for the rest of your life." I immediately understood why I was worrying about the boy. Mom had set a high bar for my behavior. I might not have liked that she disciplined me, but I knew her standards were there because she loved me.

As a Christian, you will have similar experiences. When you struggle with temptation or run in the wrong direction, the Holy Spirit is there to help. He lives in you—helping you, redirecting you, and reminding you of His standard. We need His guidance. We need to be told over and over again that God is the standard, and the standard is good. So don't be discouraged when God disciplines you. He is invested in who you are becoming and in the journey it will take for you to get there. The Lord always corrects the ones He loves.

Lord,

Thank You for your discipline. It shows that You love me. When I think about being corrected by You, I feel . . .

You have said not to take Your discipline lightly. Please forgive me for when I have seen Your discipline as . . .

I am grateful for the Holy Spirit. Today I will listen when He reminds me about . . .

It is well. Amen.

34

When Jesus had said this, he was troubled in his spirit and testified, "Truly I tell you, one of you will betray me. . . . He's the one I give the piece of bread to after I have dipped it." When he had dipped the bread, he gave it to Judas, Simon Iscariot's son.
—John 13:21, 26

I am always amazed when I think about the relationship between Jesus and Judas. Until this moment in the book of John, we have no record of Jesus treating Judas differently than He treated the other disciples. He didn't treat him like the betrayer Jesus knew he was. Instead, Jesus treated Judas with kindness, corrected him when he needed it, and loved him like He did the others. That had to be part of why the disciples were so confused.

We can learn so much from the relationship between Jesus and Judas. Jesus's love for him was real. Even with what He knew was going to happen, Jesus's love did . . . not . . . change. But the enemy attacked Judas's love for Jesus and won. This is a reminder to be careful that you don't let the enemy do the same to you. Later, Jesus's other disciples let Him down, one by one. But Jesus was committed to loving them with a love they didn't have to earn. Just as He is with you.

Lord,

Thank You for not making me work for Your love. Your relationship with Judas is an example of Your unending love for me. I want to love more like You by . . .

What I have learned about You today is . . .

Thinking about attacks from the enemy can be scary. I need to stay connected to You. Please forgive me for when I have not invested in our relationship by . . .

Judas's story shows the true love that Jesus has for His disciples. Today I will share Your love by . . .

It is well. Amen.

35

The entirety of your word is truth, each of your righteous judgments endures forever.
—Psalm 119:160

In my house we have a chore chart that I made. The kids don't have to agree with it or like it. Because I also make the rules, the chore chart stands. The same thing is true about the Bible. Because it is God's thoughts—and because the whole earth and everything in it is His—He sets the rules. The Bible is called God's Word, and it is full of His truth.

The Bible is not like God's social media account, filled with snapshots of His thoughts, filtered pics of His plans, and ads about His desires. The Bible is more like His diary. We don't have to worry about what parts are real and what are not. If someone were to read your diary, I'm sure they would know more about you than most of your friends. Why? Diaries are a space where we are the most honest. In the Bible, God shares who He is—His joys, hurts, and plans. The good thing is, He doesn't want to keep His thoughts a secret. He has made His Word available to you to read so that you can grow closer to Him.

Lord,

Thank You for giving me the Bible. Your words are true and a way for me to know You more. Learning Your Word can help grow my faith. Please forgive me for when I have been disinterested and have chosen to . . .

_____
_____
_____
_____
_____

These choices show me what I value. I want to commit to reading . . .

_____
_____
_____
_____
_____

Today I will start with . . .

_____
_____
_____
_____
_____
_____

It is well. Amen.

36

All Scripture is inspired by God and is profitable for teaching, for rebuking, for correcting, for training in righteousness, so that the man of God may be complete, equipped for every good work.
—2 Timothy 3:16-17

I was a sprinter all through high school. My coach had a rule: during the off season, the sprinters had to run on her cross country team. Cross country is running for miles, the exact opposite of the thirty to forty seconds it took me to sprint my regular races. The coach required this discipline so we would stay in shape and be ready when our season came around. She wanted us equipped and ready to race.

Like all those miles we ran each fall, the Bible helps equip us to be fully ready to do great things. Through its discipline we acquire faith, wisdom, vision for our future, and a life filled with value. Those who trust God's Word can expect to be fully ready to do good works.

There is no age requirement on good works. The Bible's proven system of discipline was used and applied in the lives of young people throughout history, often while they were still children or teenagers. David became an incredible warrior, Josiah ruled as king, Esther saved her people, Jeremiah prophesied, Joseph interpreted dreams, Joshua led an entire nation, and Mary gave birth to the Savior. Others served in ministry, were ripped from their homelands, and put their lives in danger. Their difficulties served as training. As they trusted in God and His preparation, they were all ready to do good works.

Lord,

Thank You for not allowing my age to keep me from serving You. The idea of serving You at this age makes me feel...

I am inspired by the great works of others. Forgive me for not having the courage to...

I want to be fully ready, so today I will spend time...

It is well. Amen.

37

All Scripture is inspired by God and is profitable for teaching, for rebuking, for correcting, for training in righteousness, so that the man of God may be complete, equipped for every good work.
—2 Timothy 3:16–17

Have you read *The Hunger Games* or seen the movie? After the tributes were chosen to compete in the games, they had to leave their districts to be trained in the capitol, where their tools, clothes, and training were better than anything they had ever seen. Katniss, the main character, had a bow that never seemed to run out of arrows! The tributes were taught to use their skills strategically, and they learned that fear and self-doubt were their enemies. They were being fully equipped.

In today's verse, being equipped means being provided with spiritual tools and biblical training and allowing God's Spirit to teach you how to use your gifts. I have also read it paraphrased as being "put together and shaped" (MSG), which means removing the brokenness and bad habits that hold you back. Hold you back from what? Every. Good. Work. The mission God has designed for you—the places He wants you to go, the people He wants you to serve, the relationships He wants you to cultivate, the work He wants you to enjoy, and every challenge He wants you to overcome—those are all His to choose. What an honor that He chooses and equips you for them.

Lord,

Thank You for giving me the Bible. You designed it to equip me so that I may serve You as . . .

Growing in Your Word prepares me for good works. Forgive me for how I have chosen to . . .

Today I commit to continue reading . . .

It is well. Amen.

38

"If you love me, you will keep my commands."
—John 14:15

I used to forget to take my allergy pills every day, and I would suffer for it. I began to put them out at night to remind me in the morning. It worked. The idea came from a book my boss asked me to read, *Atomic Habits*. The book's message is that goals are just words. Systems are how you get things done. You have to build a system that helps you change, and then you have to use it. As you practice your system's small habits, they eventually stick, and you begin to see change over time. My required reading did pay off; it helped me control my allergies.

God did not intend obeying His commands to be a goal. His commands are more than just words; they exist because of His love for us. God is the original system-builder. He has established ways for obedience to happen. In Matthew 22:37, Jesus says, "Love the Lord your God with all your heart, with all your soul, and with all your mind." Then He says in today's verse that if you love Him, the only proper response is to obey Him. The smallest act of obedience, multiplied over time, will produce more obedience. As you practice your love for God, you will obey His commands.

Lord,

Thank You for loving me first. Thinking about this makes me feel . . .

The way I should respond to Your love for me is . . .

Please forgive me for when I have not practiced obedience. I confess I need to work on obedience when it comes to . . .

To grow my love for You today, I will obey by . . .

It is well. Amen.

39

But godliness with contentment is great gain. For we brought nothing into the world, and we can take nothing out.
—1 Timothy 6:6–7

Why does jealousy have to be a thing? How many times have I told myself that I don't care about someone else's stuff and then realize that I can't stop thinking about it? I try to be content, but I still find myself unhappy with what I have because I have seen what she has. Even with good intentions, how do I end up in sin?

I have learned envy and greed are easy traps for me. I have had to admit just how much of my sin has been caused by comparison and entitlement. You can imagine how much this sin has impacted relationships in my life.

The Bible uses the word *covet*. It means to want something that belongs to someone else and to want it so bad that it becomes an idol. It's easy to get there when comparing our bodies, boyfriends, education, jobs, cars, clothes, money, friends, and even spiritual journeys. It can get so out of control that it spirals into sinfulness. This sinfulness is a trap. Comparison messes with our minds and steals our joy. But godliness with contentment is the key to spiritual richness and will teach us to be grateful and satisfied.

Lord,

Thank You for providing a path to contentment. I want to live a life that pleases You. As I learn about myself, I see that I am becoming . . .

Please forgive me for when I have let comparison steal my joy. I confess that I haven't been content with . . .

To work against comparison and jealousy, today I will be grateful for . . .

It is well. Amen.

40

"Do not remember the past events; pay no attention to things of old. Look, I am about to do something new; even now it is coming. Do you not see it?"
—Isaiah 43:18–19

Home makeover shows are my favorite! I love to see the before, watch the renovation, and watch the homeowners' reactions to their new place. I even began to do my own makeovers at home. For birthdays, it would be room renovations. For the holidays, room renovations. Party coming up? Boom, room renovations! What's interesting is that I have not always been a fan of change.

Change can be hard, especially when you can't immediately see the value in it. I have learned that change is at the center of our growth as people and as Christians. Nothing grows without it. Once you become a Christian, you are different than before. From then on, the Holy Spirit constantly works to mature your faith. This is a process called sanctification. If you're willing to learn, change can help you become more of who you are intended to be. You can rest easy when it comes to change; the Lord is always doing something new.

Lord,

Thank You for changing me and making me better. I want to embrace change if it makes me more like You. When I think about change in my life, I feel . . .

I understand You have a plan for my growth in You. Forgive me for when I have allowed change to . . .

Today I will be grateful for change because . . .

It is well. Amen.

LORD, here's who and what I'm praying for . . .

I'm grateful You've answered these prayers . . .

41

We know that all things work together for the good of those who love God, who are called according to his purpose.
—Romans 8:28

A friend once told me that she likes conflict. I thought it was the silliest thing I had ever heard. Who likes conflict? When I asked why, she told me she always learns something about herself when it's over. From then on, I considered her my smartest friend! That little nugget of wisdom would have a big effect on my life. It is just like the Lord to take a negative thing and use it as a good thing.

Despite what you might believe, conflict is not always bad. You can learn how strong your relationship is by how you go through and resolve conflict. For that to happen, you have to resist the temptation to be defensive, and you have to be willing to listen. Really moving forward requires everyone involved to make a commitment to honesty. God is able to use conflicts to mature you, to humble you, and to encourage you. All things—even conflict—work together for your good.

Lord,

Thank You for using so many things for my good. Even conflict can help me grow. When I experience conflict, I feel . . .

What I have learned about You is . . .

Growing from conflict can push me toward Your purpose for my life. Forgive me for how I handled conflict with . . .

The way I think about conflict has changed to . . .

It is well. Amen.

42

"See, I am the Lord's servant," said Mary. "May it happen to me as you have said." Then the angel left her.
—Luke 1:38

Mary was about fifteen years old when she found out that God was going to use her to grow a miracle who would change the world. Being a single, pregnant girl in her day would have been a huge scandal. This incredible honor could cost her everything. I am so impressed with Mary because, even at her age, God knew she was the right person for the job. I am even more impressed by her answer to God: "I am Your servant."

God is on a mission to grow you into a young woman who trusts Him, much like He grew Mary's trust. Not only was her response mind-blowing, but if you keep reading Luke 2, you will see how much she believed God. Mary was able to look ahead and see how her current, very uncomfortable situation was ultimately going to bring God glory and bless future generations. Mary was a regular person like you. But she was convinced that God was good, so saying "no" to His plan for her life was not an option.

Lord,

Thank You for Mary's brave obedience. Her example encourages me to . . .

There are times when it is hard to trust Your plan for my life. Forgive me for when I don't have the courage to . . .

I am Your servant, Lord. Today I commit to saying "yes" to . . .

It is well. Amen.

43

But be doers of the word and not hearers only, deceiving yourselves. Because if anyone is a hearer of the word and not a doer, he is like someone looking at his own face in a mirror. For he looks at himself, goes away, and immediately forgets what kind of person he was. But the one who looks intently into the perfect law of freedom and perseveres in it and is not a forgetful hearer but a doer who works—this person will be blessed in what he does.
—James 1:22-25

Have you heard of Kim Rhode? She is an Olympic skeet shooter. No woman has been more successful in the sport. At the London Olympics in 2012, Kim won gold *and* tied the world record by hitting 99 out of 100 clays. To be ready for this competition, she trained seven days a week, including the day she flew to the London Games. She used between five hundred and one thousand rounds a day, seven days a week. Her shells and targets could cost as much as $700 a day!

Kim was committed to her sport. She was so determined to be the best that she persevered even when it cost her a lot of money. Today's verse is asking you to be as committed as Kim . . . to God's Word. The Lord wants you to be so committed to His Word that you not only read it, study it, and listen to podcasts and sermons about it, but you also are motivated to do what it says. Practice is the key to your success, but practice also takes perseverance. The blessing is found in what you do over a long time.

Lord,

Thank You for giving me opportunities to experience Your blessing. As I read these verses in James, what I learned about You is . . .

Doing what Your Word says honors You. Forgive me for not committing to . . .

I want to practice being obedient, so today I commit to . . .

It is well. Amen.

44

Catch the foxes for us—the little foxes that ruin the vineyards—for our vineyards are in bloom.
—Song of Songs 2:15

I was in a book club that read a book called *Respectable Sins*. The book's goal is to help us own up to and deal with sins that are subtle or less dramatic. It has become normal to judge some sins as worse than others. We use words like *major sin* for all the "big" sins that would publicly embarrass us or our families. Doing this makes it easy to look at other sins as "smaller," which allows us to feel not as bad about them hanging around our lives.

But sin is like drug use. It's costly, and it only takes a little to do a lot of damage. Sin is also dangerous. It leaves us by ourselves when we're not okay and we need help. Sin is the leading cause of all deaths! Our sins are offensive to God and damaging to our spiritual growth. Being in denial about sins that are considered "acceptable" to our friends is disloyal to God. As today's verse says, it only takes a little fox to come and ruin a blooming vineyard. Our small sins can cause big problems if we let them.

Lord,

Thank You for teaching me to be on guard against the sin in my life. All sin betrays You. As I read today's verse, I am aware that I . . .

Sins that seem the smallest can often be the most dangerous. Forgive me for not being careful about . . .

In response to Your warning, I commit to no longer be okay with . . .

It is well. Amen.

45

For the word of God is living and effective and sharper than any double-edged sword, penetrating as far as the separation of soul and spirit, joints and marrow. It is able to judge the thoughts and intentions of the heart.
—Hebrews 4:12

I am married to a rapper. (That's my favorite icebreaker when I meet new people.) He was part of a group that performed at thousands of concerts together. One of my favorite parts was when the concert was over. After the music had ended and the crowds thinned out, a few people would get backstage, green-room access to their favorite rappers. They would be so excited, taking pictures and getting autographs. Some asked for advice, and others shared their stories. All of them wanted to make the most of the special access they had been granted.

The Bible is like having your own all-access, VIP pass into the mind of God. It is full of promises you can trust. It has answers for best friends and broken relationships. It can make sisters out of enemies and family out of strangers. God gives His people a new identity, and the Bible helps us understand it. His Word declares you are His daughter and His masterpiece, created to do good works. The Bible has tools for you to live with boldness, strength, wisdom, joy, dignity, and compassion. Please don't take it for granted; make the most of the life-giving access you have been given.

Lord,

The Bible is full of answers to change my life. Thank You for giving me more access to You through it. I have always thought taking time to read the Bible was . . .

_____
_____
_____
_____
_____

Today's verse reminds me that Your words are powerful and relevant. Forgive me for treating You . . .

_____
_____
_____
_____
_____

Because of the access I have to You through Your Word, today I commit to read . . .

_____
_____
_____
_____
_____

It is well. Amen.

46

Let the whole earth shout triumphantly to the LORD! Serve the LORD with gladness; come before him with joyful songs. Acknowledge that the LORD is God. He made us, and we are his—his people, the sheep of his pasture. Enter his gates with thanksgiving and his courts with praise. Give thanks to him and bless his name. For the LORD is good, and his faithful love endures forever; his faithfulness, through all generations.
—PSALM 100

I grew up in a church that loved to sing to the Lord. Our large choir was always exciting. I loved to listen to the older ladies sing. They always sang like they spent time with Jesus. Sunday mornings taught me what it looks like to serve the Lord with gladness, to come before Him with joyful songs, thanksgiving, and praise. Being in a community that modeled these things gave me the foundation my faith is built on today.

Today's verses are a psalm of thanksgiving, written for the entire world. The writer wants us to remember *why* we praise the Lord and to teach us *how*. The "why" is because God made us, and we are His! The Lord is the definition of good, and He offers His love to us forever! The "how" is done by being glad to serve Him and singing joyful songs to Him. It's acknowledging that He is the only true God and giving Him the thanks He deserves. Doing these things can help push out our idols. Being reminded of the "Godness" of God should put a song in our hearts instead, a song that tells the world around us that we have been with Him.

Lord,

Thank You for reminding me how big You are. Being thankful is the right response. When I imagine the whole earth praising You, I feel . . .

Remembering how good You are is humbling. Forgive me for not acknowledging this when . . .

Today I will focus on the things that I have to be thankful for, like . . .

It is well. Amen.

47

"You did not choose me, but I chose you. I appointed you to go and produce fruit and that your fruit should remain, so that whatever you ask the Father in my name, he will give you."
—John 15:16–17

A few years ago, I would have said that growing up without my father in my home did not affect me at all. But the truth is, I was impacted. As the oldest child, I had to help my mom lead. I secretly resented my father for leaving us. Living without him hurt, especially when he wasn't there to protect me, let me cry on him, or scare away annoying boys. These hurts eventually became emotional walls that I put up to defend myself. Honestly, they were less like walls and more like fortresses.

Jesus chose us, and He wants us to produce lots of fruit in Him. But the wounds we may be nursing can distract us and keep us from enjoying the benefits He provides. I had unknowingly allowed my dad's absence to define me. I believed I was unworthy, unimportant, and unwanted. I transferred this broken thinking to my relationship with God. How could I trust any father, including God, to take care of me? Today's verse encouraged me. I wanted to live like He had chosen me. So I decided to ask God to help me trust Him more and to help me eventually be healed from the hurt. He has done both. If you've had practice building your own walls (or fortresses), remember that you can ask God to help you, and He will hear you.

Lord,

Thank You for choosing me and producing fruit in me. When I think about how distracting it can be to focus only on my wounds, I feel ...

You can use the pain in my life to produce fruit that remains. Please forgive me for when I have allowed my hurts to ...

Today I ask You to heal me of ...

It is well. Amen.

48

Who among you is wise and understanding? By his good conduct he should show that his works are done in the gentleness that comes from wisdom.
—JAMES 3:13

What do you think makes someone wise? I have always thought of wisdom as the answers you get from old people. After spending quality time with a few elderly friends at church, I know there is some truth in that. Asking Siri for an answer just doesn't compare to trusting the years of experience our parents or grandparents have. Instead of judging wisdom by age, our society often assumes that if a person has a lot of money or education then they must be wise. But we have all seen how people who are really rich or super smart can still easily make bad choices.

James liked the way the Old Testament talks about wisdom. If you read about it in books like Psalms and Proverbs, you can see that wisdom is a way of life. It describes how the wise person behaves and makes everyday decisions. Wise people today are not usually associated with words like gentleness. But James says that is the way to identify those who are wise and understanding. If you want to be wise, spend time with wise people. To find them, watch how they live.

Lord,

Thank You for showing me that wisdom means more than having money or being successful in the world. It is a way of life. Today's verse describes a wise person. Someone this makes me think of is . . .

You want me to live a life of wisdom. Please forgive me for when I have not. I confess that I . . .

Today I will pray for a wise person in my life like . . .

It is well. Amen.

49

*Be gracious to me, Lord, for I am weak;
heal me, Lord, for my bones are shaking.*
—Psalm 6:2

Kirtsugi is a Japanese art form where artists take broken pottery pieces and glue them back together with gold and lacquer. When they are done, the bowl or cup has beautiful gold lines showing off where the breaks used to be. The purpose is to show how the pottery can become more beautiful because it has experienced being broken. David, the writer of today's psalm, can relate to this. This entire psalm is him begging God to take away his pain. Brokenness had become the backdrop to so much of David's life.

All of us have broken pieces in our stories. A friend of mine named Steph keeps having hard things happen to her. She just graduated from college, but nothing she planned seems to be working out. Having to move back home with her parents has her feeling defeated. But God is gracious even in our weakness. He hears us when we cry. Steph knows these two truths, so she has continued to pray for help. Recently, when I checked in with her, she had been invited to a kintsugi event. Through it, she has begun to see how God is using this hard season to make her more beautiful.

Lord,

Thank You for being gracious to me even in my weakness. You have invited me to come to You when I am hurting. Doing that makes me feel . . .

David made praying a big part of his life. Something that keeps me from having a habit of prayer is . . .

Please forgive me for this. You will use the brokenness in my story. Today I am grateful for . . .

It is well. Amen.

50

Love must be sincere. Hate what is evil; cling to what is good.
—Romans 12:9 niv

It's funny how siblings can grow up in the same house and be so very different. They all know what is expected of them, yet some of them live like they don't care about the rules. This was true of me and my sister. Every day, our choices showed our mother what we believed about the rules she set in our home. One of us was known for going against the rules and getting in trouble, and the other was the opposite. Our mother made it clear that although she loved us the same, our decisions meant she had to discipline us differently.

Notice that the commands in today's verse are in present tense. Paul, the author of Romans, is reminding us that we are responsible for our choices. The Lord has made it clear how we are to live. We are supposed to avoid things that will lead to harm and hold on to the things that He has taught us are good. You can understand the difference by reading the Bible, learning at church, and spending time with other Christians. When you love these things, it's proof you are maturing in life and growing in your faith.

Lord,

Thank You that Your love for me is sincere. You have proven this to me by . . .

That makes me feel . . .

This verse has commands that I know I have broken. Please forgive me for . . .

You have told me to cling to what is good. Today I choose to . . .

It is well. Amen.

LORD, here's who and what I'm praying for...

I'm grateful You've answered these prayers . . .

51

Therefore, be imitators of God, as dearly loved children.
—Ephesians 5:1

A friend of mine watches a show about a big family living on a huge farm. The mom and dad decided their nine children would live without much influence from the world around them, so they are homeschooled, do all the church activities, and don't watch TV. They have never tasted soda or candy!

The oldest son married a girl who doesn't respect the way his parents do things. She introduced him to soda, movies, and lots of other things. She has also tried to do the same thing with his younger siblings. Her desire to "help them have experiences" goes against the rules of their parents and creates conflict in their family. This son is forced to choose between the unique lifestyle of his parents' home and his wife's ideas.

You may never live on a farm or choose not to have a TV, but God does call you to have a set-apart identity. If you haven't already, you will one day be presented with lifestyle choices that others say are great. How will you respond? Will you imitate God? Sometimes even good opportunities may not be what is best for you. What you will need is commitment, courage, and community with accountability to be sure your choices match who you are—a daughter of God.

LORD,

Thank You for loving me as Your child. What I am learning about Your love for me is . . .

That makes me feel . . .

Today's verse teaches me to imitate You. Please forgive me for when I have . . .

I want to look like You for others to see. Today I will . . .

IT IS WELL. AMEN.

52

God is our refuge and strength, a very present help in trouble.
—Psalm 46:1 ESV

When we truly believe something, it changes us. Whether big or small, the changes show what we have been convinced by, what we trust. When you trust the dentist, you take care of your teeth. When you believe in kindness, you treat people kindly. And when you believe God, it changes your whole life. I used to think I had to be strong enough to control all the things going on in my life. But when things went bad—when I developed asthma as an athlete or when both my grandmothers died—I realized that my strength was actually weak. I became convinced of my need for help.

On my wall, I have a quote by an author named John Maxwell. It says, "You cannot always control what happens to you, but you can control what happens in you." Hard things will happen. You may get a tough diagnosis, you may lose relationships, someone you trust may lie to you, or you might experience abuse, abandonment, or rejection. All those things happened to me but what happened *in* me was special. By praying and building a relationship with God, my pain began healing and my fears started going away. He gave me courage to speak up and to forgive. I found safety in Him. The things that happened to me showed me how to live as the new me, looking to God as my refuge and strength.

LORD,

Thank You for being my strength. What I am learning about You is . . .

You have said that You offer help when I am in trouble. Please forgive me for when I have not come to You about . . .

I want to change what happens in me. Today I will . . .

IT IS WELL. AMEN.

53

Let us run with endurance the race that lies before us, keeping our eyes on Jesus, the pioneer and perfecter of our faith.
—Hebrews 12:1-2

"You are good, but you're not on the level that we need." I have heard those words a few times in my life. Sometimes they motivated me, like when I was determined to be on the All-City Jazz Band. Other times they deflated me, like when I gave up playing tennis because I was clearly no good at it. The words "not on the level" stuck with me. I thought back to them often, especially when I was insecure and began to question where I was in life. I even measured how good a Christian I was based on what I saw in other people.

Have you ever compared your faith journey with someone else's? Have you wondered why you're not at the same place spiritually that other people are? If so, today's verse says to keep your eyes on Jesus. There will always be people who seem to pray better, know more, or have more courage to share their faith than you. You may have friends who are so committed to Jesus that their faith makes you question your own. Every Christian grows at her own pace. You don't need to be discouraged by someone else's "level." Be dedicated to running your race. Focus on Jesus, and you will grow to new levels at the pace He sets for you.

Lord,

Thank You for giving me my own race to run. Believing those words is a choice, and I choose . . .

You tell me to run with endurance. Please forgive me for when I have given up and . . .

Today I will keep my eyes on You by . . .

It is well. Amen.

54

Jesus replied, "Truly I tell you, unless someone is born again, he cannot see the kingdom of God."
—John 3:3

When you were born, you became someone's child. When you are born again, you become God's child. This happens the moment you realize that you need forgiveness, admit to being sinful, and apologize to God. Then your heart is changed, and, hopefully, you want to live your life differently. Your first birth was physical; this second birth is spiritual.

There are people who have grown up in Christian homes and communities and heard the truth of Jesus Christ for years, but they have never believed. Others may give them credit for being a Christian, and some may have even fooled themselves. In his book *Am I Really a Christian?*, Mike McKinley writes about the Bible's description of faith in Christ. He says you are not a Christian just because you say you are or just because you like Jesus. You're also not a Christian if you enjoy sin, love your stuff, or don't love other people. You are a Christian if you have been born again.

Lord,

Thank You for allowing me to be born again in You. Because of this, I am Your child forever. The fact that I belong to You makes me feel . . .

My second spiritual birth happened when I became a Christian and acknowledged my need for forgiveness. Today I need to be forgiven for . . .

Being a Christian means that I want to live differently than I used to. Today I make the decision to . . .

It is well. Amen.

55

*May the words of my mouth and the meditation of my heart
be acceptable to you, Lord, my rock and my Redeemer.*
—Psalm 19:14

Some of the most important changes in history have happened because of words. Martin Luther King Jr.'s "I Have a Dream" speech helped to promote unity and civil rights for everyone. Long before that, Moses spoke with God and was given the Ten Commandments to guide God's people. And in the beginning, God used His words to bring the entire world into existence. Though our words may not shape human history, they do show what is in our hearts, and they do affect those around us.

I have today's verse memorized and say it all the time. It's a prayer that reminds me how important it is to please God with my thoughts and words. Growing up, my pastor ended every church service by reciting this psalm. He prayed the words over us to inspire us to respect God with every part of our lives. Let this prayer inspire you too, so that the words you allow in your mind and those you speak through your mouth are ones that please the Lord.

Lord,

Thank You for being my Rock and my Redeemer. These words show me that You and I can have a relationship. The other thing I have learned about You today is . . .

The words in my mind and in my mouth should make You proud. Please forgive me for when I have thought or talked about . . .

What I am learning about myself is . . .

Today I will use my words to . . .

It is well. Amen.

56

I am amazed that you are so quickly turning away from him who called you by the grace of Christ and are turning to a different gospel—not that there is another gospel, but there are some who are troubling you and want to distort the gospel of Christ.
—Galatians 1:6-7

I have a friend who is known for being into designer clothes and wanting the best of everything. I call her my "high-end friend." One of the first things people notice is her huge diamond wedding ring. But when she went to get insurance on the ring, she found out the diamond was not real! My high-end friend who loves beautiful things did not spot that fake. If you're not trained to know what the real thing looks like, it's easy to accept the fake things as real.

False prophets are people who take what is true about God and twist it. They offer pieces of the truth and wrap them in lies to make them look like "diamonds." We need to be trained to recognize what is bogus so that we can grow in what is real. Then we will avoid turning to another gospel. The more partial truths seep into your faith, the less you will look and act like Jesus. Fake diamonds may shine like real ones, buy they don't fool those who have learned to recognize what's genuine.

LORD,

Thank You for wanting me to know the truth about You. You want me to know You so that I won't be tricked by lies about You. Forgive me for when I choose to listen to . . .

I don't want to turn away from You. Please help me to . . .

Today my prayer for my faith journey is . . .

IT IS WELL. AMEN.

57

Consider it a great joy, my brothers and sisters, whenever you experience various trials, because you know that the testing of your faith produces endurance. And let endurance have its full effect, so that you may be mature and complete, lacking nothing.
—James 1:2-4

When my son, Jay, was in eleventh grade, we moved to another state. Although his new school was nice and our new city was beautiful, he was apprehensive about starting over, trying to fit in, and finding new friends. He had gone to a small school where he knew everyone. The new school had thousands of students. He felt invisible. Even after going to the school for a year, he found it hard to make relationships.

It felt like Jay was becoming less and less like the fun, outgoing guy we all knew him to be. One day he shared with me how hard the move had really been. He felt out of place and uncomfortable. As a Christian, he didn't understand why Jesus would allow this struggle.

The words in today's verse bring hope. Tough times in your life are trials. They test your faith to grow your spiritual strength. Even Jesus was tested (Matthew 4:1-11)! Trials often take something away. When they do, the Lord wants you to be able to trust Him to give you exactly what you need. This was the reminder Jay needed to find his joy again.

Lord,

Thank You for using hard things in my life to make me stronger. None of it is a waste of time. When I think about how You have used my hard things, I feel . . .

You want me to have an authentic faith in You. Forgive me for when I have doubted that You . . .

I want to endure trials like Jesus did. He talked to You and repeated Your words. I will start doing this by . . .

Today I am asking You to help me find joy in . . .

It is well. Amen.

58

"You pore over the Scriptures because you think you have eternal life in them, and yet they testify about me."
—John 5:39

When we pick up a book, we are often not neutral. We might have thoughts about the writer, the type of book it is, or reviews we have heard. Reading the Bible is the same way. You bring to it things you have already learned in church, the way you see the world, your life experiences, and what you think about God. These thoughts shape your expectations. So you might read the Bible looking for God to validate you or your choices. Sometimes you'll be looking for an emotional jolt of peace, joy, or patience. Or you may just want to be told what to do.

God intended for the Bible to tell us about Him. His Word invites us into the bigness of who He is. All of Scripture is about God, so when we read it, our first question should be, "What does this teach me about who God is?" Yes, there are answers for you, and there is hope for your situation, but all of it comes from God, who is your teacher, protector, healer, and provider. No wonder the Bible is still the most popular book of all time.

Lord,

Thank You for giving me the chance to really understand You. The Bible is Your gift to me. Please forgive me for when I may have only opened it to get . . .

You want me to read the Bible to learn about You. What I have learned today is . . .

To learn more about You today, I will read . . .

It is well. Amen.

59

Be gracious to me, God, according to your faithful love; according to your abundant compassion, blot out my rebellion. Completely wash away my guilt and cleanse me from my sin.
—Psalm 51:1-2

I remember getting caught. I was in preschool and had stolen a coin from a girl in my class. I can't even tell you why I did it, but my mom was not happy when she found out. We both knew that was not the first or last time I would embarrass her with my sinfulness, but somehow I knew my mom would forgive me. When I became a Christian, the confidence I had in receiving forgiveness changed. I struggled to believe God would be willing to forgive me, over and over again, for the rest of my life.

Today's verses are words from David, a person who had a close relationship with the Lord and still messed up. He was a king, so when he made terrible mistakes, the consequences were huge. But he was still able to bring his faults to God because of what he knew about Him. David was humble enough to see that he needed forgiveness, and he was confident that God was willing to give it to him.

Psalm 51 has been called "the mirror psalm" because it reflects a heart that is transparent, truly apologetic, and willing to be disciplined. Does your heart look like David's? When God made you, He knew you would need His forgiveness. The question is, are you willing to accept it?

Lord,

Thank You for forgiving me. Because of Jesus, You don't see a bad person when You look at me. Thinking about Your forgiveness makes me feel ...

Today I ask You to forgive me for ...

What I am learning about my faith in You is ...

It is well. Amen.

60

And let us consider one another in order to provoke love and good works, not neglecting to gather together, as some are in the habit of doing, but encouraging each other.
—Hebrews 10:24-25

On an international prayer Zoom call, I met a twenty-year-old woman who lived on the other side of the world. She loved being on these calls because she didn't know of another Christian within two hundred miles of where she lived. The faraway friends on the call had become her Christian family, building a sisterhood that stretches around the globe. God designed that young woman to need others. This is true of everybody: we all need people.

In his book *Radical*, David Platt says, "We are settling for a Christianity that revolves around catering to ourselves when the central message of Christianity is actually about abandoning ourselves." Sometimes it's easy to have a selfish Christianity, one that focuses on my quiet time, my prayer life, or my small group instead of the needs of the people around me. Your salvation is personal, but your faith journey is supposed to be shared with others. You are being built up as part of a Christian community, one God put in place for you to discover. It is His plan for the many to serve together as one.

Lord,

Thank You for creating me to be part of something bigger than me. A selfish faith is the opposite of Your design. Forgive me for when I have chosen to focus on ...

Being a part of a Christian community is good for me. When I think about that blessing, it makes me feel ...

Today I pray that my community will ...

It is well. Amen.

LORD, here's who and what I'm praying for . . .

I'm grateful You've answered these prayers . . .

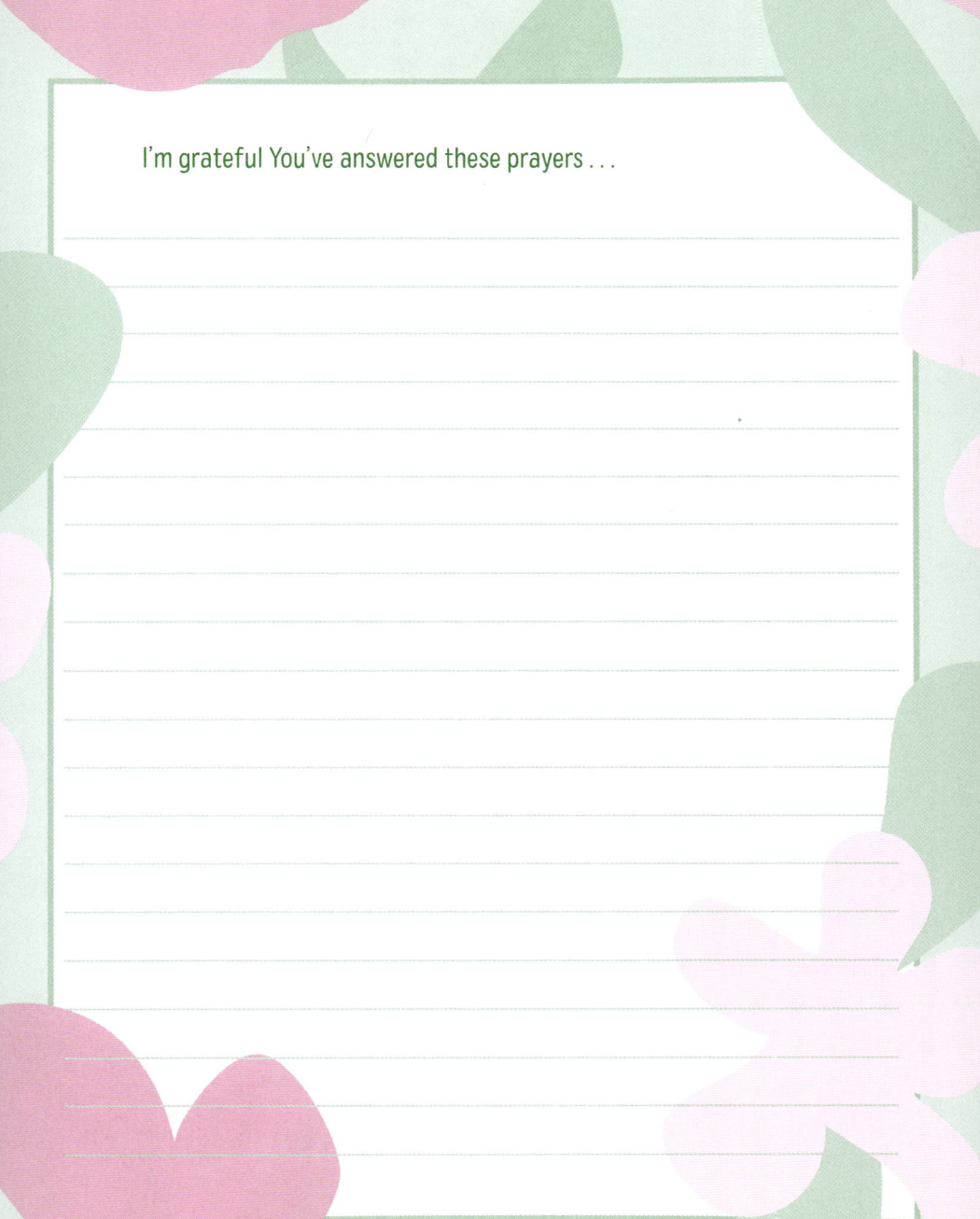

61

Therefore, my dear friends, just as you have always obeyed, so now, not only in my presence but even more in my absence, work out your own salvation with fear and trembling.
—Philippians 2:12

I imagine when you hear the word *exercise* you think P. E. class, burpees, or treadmills. That makes perfect sense. But *exercise* also means to put to use or to make something happen. Like when people exercise their right to vote. They put their voting rights to good use, making the election process happen. So one kind of exercising means *you* are working out, and another kind means you are working *stuff* out.

Today's verse reminds us of our responsibility to pay attention to how we live each day because of the salvation we've been given. To work out your salvation is to show appreciation for it. It's always nice to hear someone say "thank you" for a gift, but it is even nicer to see them enjoying it. God wants you to show Him and those around you that you are grateful for your salvation by enjoying it, by exercising the behavior and attitudes that Jesus did. The part about fear and trembling is not about being afraid of God but about having respect for Him. All exercise takes work. One kind will build up your body, but spiritual exercise will build up your life.

LORD,

Thank You for saving me. My life is different now because of You, and I am grateful. The best part about being Yours is . . .

Sometimes I forget to show my gratitude. Forgive me for when I am ungrateful and I . . .

Today I will try to work out my salvation by . . .

IT IS WELL. AMEN.

62

So he got up from supper, laid aside his outer clothing, took a towel, and tied it around himself. Next, he poured water into a basin and began to wash his disciples' feet and to dry them with the towel tied around him.
—John 13:4–5

When my husband and I got married, we were young and broke. So were our friends. Even after our guy friends agreed to be in the wedding, it was clear right away that they could not afford suits. Well, my husband and I decided to nix the entire bridal party because, for us, it was more important to have them at the wedding than in it.

Later, our girl friends got together and gifted us the money they had used to hold their bridesmaids' dresses. They wanted to make our day great. It was a sacrifice for them, but they loved us. Our friends served us without expecting anything in return. Their display of love was so impactful to me. That humble yet generous gesture pointed me and my soon-to-be husband to Jesus.

In today's verses Jesus is washing the disciples' feet. He took a low position with the friends He loved so that He could model something else He loved—service. His entire life was about serving others. Like my friends' money when we needed it or like when a family has a baby and everybody brings a meal, Jesus's love is always in service to others. His expectation is that you, as His disciple, will do the same.

Lord,

Thank You for not just telling me to serve but for modeling it. Your example encourages me to . . .

Regularly serving others can be a challenge. Please forgive me for not prioritizing service when I . . .

My commitment today is to serve by . . .

It is well. Amen.

63

*"For your Father knows what you need before
you ask him. Pray then like this. . . ."*
—Matthew 6:8–9 esv

Have you heard of the Sermon on the Mount? It is Jesus's most famous sermon. In Matthew 5–7, He gives a guide for life. Right smack in the middle of the sermon, Jesus focuses on how to pray. This is where we find the "Lord's Prayer," Jesus's model for how His disciples should pray. What we learn from this is beautiful: the sweet gift of prayer is not a command, but an invitation.

My church used to sing an old hymn that says, "Just a little talk with Jesus makes it right." Jesus's disciples were able to sit and talk with Him in the flesh. Today we have His Spirit, and we get to talk to Jesus through prayer. You have been invited. My prayer is that you will pray as God called you to pray. Without performing. Not for attention. Not because you are required to. But by living out your faith every day in the truth God has given you. You can pray to Him. Will you accept His invitation?

Lord,

Thank You for inviting me into a relationship with You. No one knows me better. Admitting that makes me feel . . .

I want to really know how to pray. Forgive me for treating prayer like . . .

I am now on a prayer journey with You. Today I ask You to . . .

It is well. Amen.

64

"Whenever you pray, you must not be like the hypocrites, because they love to pray standing in the synagogues and on the street corners to be seen by people. Truly I tell you, they have their reward."
—Matthew 6:5

In 1 Samuel there's a story about a woman named Hannah. Every year she and her family went to worship and offer sacrifices to the Lord at Shiloh, where the temple was. Hannah could not have babies, but her husband's second wife, Peninnah, could. Hannah would cry and refuse to eat, but then she would go and pray.

One year, Hannah just couldn't take it anymore. She went into the temple to talk to the Lord and prayed so passionately that the high priest thought she was drunk! Her prayers were secret, and eventually, God rewarded her. The baby Hannah humbly prayed for was given to her! Her son, Samuel, became a prophet for God and a powerful judge, priest, and military leader in Israel.

Your prayers should be humble, sincere, and from your heart like Hannah's were. Not like people who want to be seen, or to make people think you are more spiritual than you are. Hannah did not pray to show off. She prayed to ask God for what she wanted, and her private time with the Lord then became a great example for us today.

Lord,

Thank You for letting Hannah be an example for me. The way she prayed encourages me to . . .

Praying with the wrong motives is a terrible way to talk to You. Please forgive me when I . . .

I have seen that the way I pray is important. My commitment today is to be careful about . . .

It is well. Amen.

65

*"Therefore, you should pray like this: Our Father in heaven,
your name be honored as holy. Your kingdom come.
Your will be done on earth as it is in heaven."*
—Matthew 6:9-10

Some people need reminders to clean up after themselves, eat healthier food, or spend their money carefully. They don't just take care of these things on their own. Sound like you at all? I promise I'm not judging. Sin has made it easy to choose what is not good for us. Everyone could use reminders to choose what is good, so when the Bible tells us to do something, it's probably because we would not naturally do it on our own.

Today's verses are an example of a reminder. Jesus used these words to teach prayer to His disciples. He began the prayer with worship. God the Son acknowledged the greatness of God the Father's position (He is in heaven), His name (honored as holy), and His plan (Your will be done).

Jesus's model prayer teaches us to start our prayers the same way. Be careful not to go into prayer time like we would a McDonald's—casually, thinking about what we want, and expecting to get out quickly. Prayer is special. It is our opportunity to experience God, and our worship draws us in so we can.

Lord,

Thank You for being a God who is good and deserves our worship. Today I want to worship You for . . .

_____
_____
_____
_____

Jesus, You have shown me how I should pray. Please forgive me when I come thinking first about . . .

_____
_____
_____
_____

How I pray is as important as *why* I pray. When I pray, I will remember to . . .

_____
_____
_____
_____

It is well. Amen.

66

"Give us today our daily bread."
—Matthew 6:11

For a long time, my mom did not have a car. We depended on buses, trains, and rides from friends to get where we needed to go. On Sundays, we took two buses to get to church. To get to my high school, I took a bus and two trains. If the bus ran late, I would miss my train and would have to wait for the next one, which could make me late for school. I had to depend on someone other than myself to get me where I needed to be. And that was often hard.

Today's verse is about dependence, and this type is definitely harder than waiting for a bus! Jesus is showing how He totally depends on the Father. He wants you to do the same. Why? First, prayer is the time to tell God what you need. He hears you and is able to meet that need. This habit builds in you the humility to ask. Second, copying Jesus always leads to blessings. And third, the more you lean on God, the more confidence you'll have in what He can do. He is never surprised by your neediness. In fact, He is drawn to your dependance on Him.

Lord,

Thank You for wanting me to lean on You. When I think about what that means, I feel . . .

Jesus was willing to be totally dependent on You. Forgive me, please, for not letting You handle . . .

What I have learned about You today is . . .

Today, *depending* will mean . . .

It is well. Amen.

67

"And forgive us our debts, as we also have forgiven our debtors."
—Matthew 6:12

Sometimes, forgiveness feels like a terrifying task that requires more than I have to give. But forgiveness clearly is important to Jesus, so it has to be a priority for me. Forgiveness started in Genesis when God promised a Redeemer, and it has been a constant theme from there. Esau forgave Jacob, Joseph forgave his brothers, God forgave Israel, David forgave Saul, Jesus forgave the woman at the well, the dad forgave his prodigal son, the master forgave the servant with the huge debt, and then there's Jesus's ultimate act of forgiveness on the cross.

In today's verse, forgiving a debt is like making the last payment on a huge loan. It cost a lot, it may not have been easy, but now that the bill has been paid, it's gone. No one can demand more money for that loan again. God used His overflowing-mercy account to pay your debt. That type of forgiveness is yours. In this part of Jesus's prayer, Jesus is teaching you to ask God for permission to draw from His mercy account so that you can do the same for someone else.

Lord,

Thank You for forgiving my debts. I know it cost You a lot. When I think about that, I feel . . .

_____
_____
_____
_____

Jesus, You are teaching me what it means to forgive others. Please forgive me for not leaning on You to forgive . . .

_____
_____
_____
_____

Your kindness to me is more than I may ever be able to understand. But today I accept it and will use it to . . .

_____
_____
_____
_____

It is well. Amen.

68

*"And do not bring us into temptation,
but deliver us from the evil one."*
—Matthew 6:13

Later in Jesus's ministry, He went to pray. He told His disciples to "stay awake and pray, so that you won't enter into temptation. The spirit is willing, but the flesh is weak" (Matthew 26:41).

Because I face temptation every day, I get what Jesus was saying. Some days I want to watch what I shouldn't watch or go places where I don't belong. I used to think temptations were mini tests that I needed to pass to please God. I'm glad that's not true because my "temptation GPA" would be so embarrassing! God is not spending His time waiting to see if I will fail; He wants to see me succeed.

In today's verse, Jesus was teaching His disciples to pray for protection. He knew that dark things are real. Every day, we are in a spiritual battle. Opportunities to do wrong are always within our reach. God wants us to recognize the danger that is inside us and all around us. If you are wise, you will ask God to protect you from being caught in the trap that temptation sets and from being tricked by the evil one's plans.

LORD,

Thank You for offering me Your protection. You want to see me succeed. When I think about that, I feel . . .

Jesus is teaching me to come to You for protection. Please forgive me when I have decided to get it from . . .

Temptation is real, but so are You. Today I will come to You when I feel tempted to . . .

IT IS WELL. AMEN.

69

Yours, O Lord, is the greatness and the power and the glory and the victory and the majesty, for all that is in the heavens and in the earth is yours. Yours is the kingdom, O Lord, and you are exalted as head above all.
—1 Chronicles 29:11 esv

When I was a kid, I wanted to be either a lawyer or a forensic scientist. I guess those choices came from my love of a good mystery and knowing random facts. It may sound boring, but you never know when you will be asked about the total number of minutes in a year. Anyway, when I started studying the Bible, my love for research and facts came in handy. One thing I have noticed is how similar today's verse is to the end of the Lord's Prayer in Matthew 6. That makes me think that a focus on the Lord and His greatness is a primary ingredient for growing our prayer lives.

In Jesus's instructions on prayer in Matthew 6, He focuses more on what the Lord can do for us than on a long list of requests. Matthew 6 and the verse in 1 Chronicles were written to point you to the absolute "Godness" of who God is and to develop in you the habit of giving Him praise. He is everything described in today's verse and more! And He is the one hearing and answering your prayers. Ending your prayer time by repeating truths about who God is can only help you grow more secure in your faith.

Lord,

Thank You for how amazing You are. You deserve my praise because You have . . .

Remembering this makes me feel . . .

I am learning so much about how to pray. Please forgive me when I . . .

The praiseworthy words that come to mind when I think about You are . . .

It is well. Amen.

70

And there was a prophetess, Anna, the daughter of Phanuel, of the tribe of Asher. . . . and then as a widow until she was eighty-four. She did not depart from the temple, worshiping with fasting and prayer night and day.
—Luke 2:36–37 ESV

I can't help but think of certain people in the Bible as superheroes. Their stories are so important that we read about them thousands of years later. Anna is one of those people. God even chose to speak through her. Like the rest of the children of Israel, she was waiting for the promised Messiah and the salvation He would bring. She must have really believed He was coming because she prayed and fasted regularly for more than sixty years.

Jesus also modeled fasting for us. He fasted for forty days and forty nights because He was being obedient to God. Jesus taught His disciples to fast as well. But why would God expect anyone to fast? Good question. Fasting is a choice to deny yourself. Jesus knows that self-denial changes us spiritually. For you, fasting may have nothing to do with food. You may need to fast from a show, a person, an app—or maybe all three—but learning to limit yourself can be effective. The beauty of fasting is that it will always do its work from the inside out.

Lord,

Thank You for the examples of great women like Anna. She trusted You to keep Your promise. Thinking about fasting makes me feel . . .

I need to learn to deny myself. Forgive me for being slow to give up . . .

Before I start fasting, I will get advice and accountability from . . .

But today I will pray for the courage to be obedient by . . .

It is well. Amen.

LORD, here's who and what I'm praying for...

I'm grateful You've answered these prayers . . .

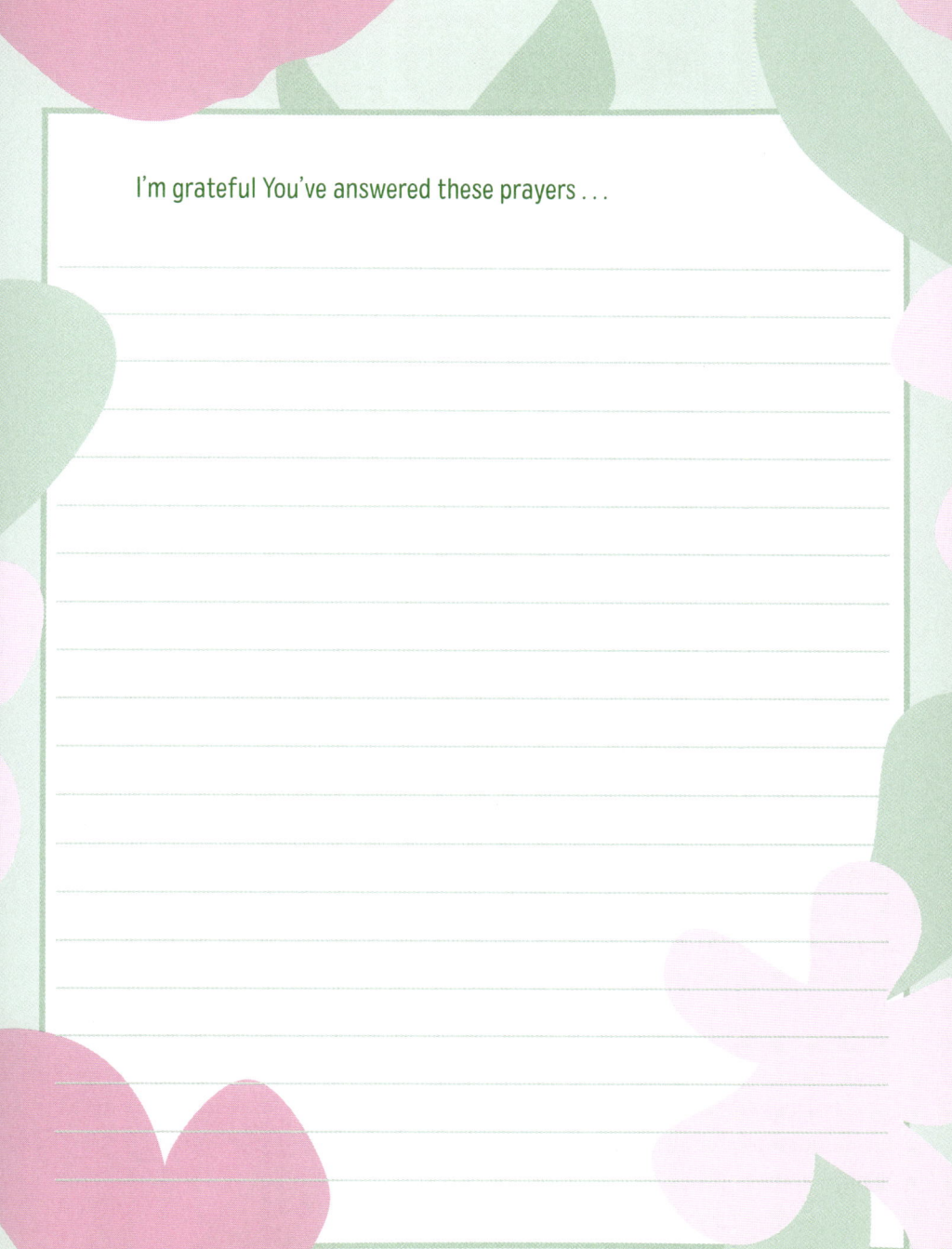

71

Blessed is the one whose transgression is forgiven, whose sin is covered. Blessed is the man against whom the L̲ord counts no iniquity, and in whose spirit there is no deceit. For when I kept silent, my bones wasted away through my groaning all day long. . . . I acknowledged my sin to you, and I did not cover my iniquity; I said, "I will confess my transgressions to the L̲ord."
—Psalm 32:1–3, 5 esv

I love documentaries. I just watched one about a mom who wanted a chance to talk to the man who had caused her son's death. She wanted to understand why. They did meet, and after they talked, he said he felt like a weight had been lifted off his shoulders. Amazingly, the mom forgave him and then became his mentor. She had wanted answers, but he found relief. Even after being convicted and spending ten years in prison, he felt better after he confessed. That story made me think.

Have you ever wondered why we still confess our sins to God when we are already forgiven? According to today's verses, He has chosen not to count our sins against us. Yet, when David, the writer of today's psalm, hid his sins, he felt terrible. Like the man in prison, his confession brought him peace. The Lord already knows what you have done, and He has forgiven you for all of it. But He also knows that admitting the truth to Him brings healing. Jesus has graciously covered your sins so that you don't have to.

Lord,

It's hard to understand that You don't hold my faults against me. Thank You for Your unbelievable forgiveness. What I have learned about You is . . .

_____
_____
_____
_____

Being honest with You about things I've done can be scary. Please forgive me for not coming to You about . . .

_____
_____
_____
_____

Confessing that to You makes me feel . . .

_____
_____
_____
_____

Today, no matter what mistakes I make, I will . . .

_____
_____
_____

It is well. Amen.

72

Little children, let us not love in word or speech, but in action and in truth.
—1 John 3:18

I used to lie to my friends to hide how broke my family was. I was embarrassed, so I lied about all kinds of things in my life: my house, my bedroom, what I ate, where I was all weekend (#justinchurchwithmom), and new things I got. I was already a Christian, and I did Christian things—like going to church, praying, and reading my Bible—but I was still living this double life. Then my pastor decided to spend a few Sundays answering the question, "What is a Christian?" I knew things in my life had to change.

To be a Christian is to be like Jesus. It means following His commands, and it also means copying His character. Jesus values everybody. He is generous, kind, and forgiving. He has patience, loves people, and values the truth.

Today's verse says that people who follow Jesus love like He does—with their actions and in truth. When we express love with integrity, or truthfulness, in ways others can see, we reflect Jesus. When I lied about my life, I was not valuing truth as Jesus does. I was not copying that part of His character. People say imitation is the highest form of flattery, which means that doing what others do is a way to show you like and value them. Whose character are you copying?

Lord,

Thank You for having high expectations for me. They push me to care about all parts of my life. Being like You means living like You. Please forgive me for being okay with . . .

Working on my character takes work. An area in my life I can focus on is . . .

Today, my first step will be . . .

It is well. Amen.

73

Jesus replied: "'Love the Lord your God with all your heart and with all your soul and with all your mind.' This is the first and greatest commandment. And the second is like it: 'Love your neighbor as yourself.' All the Law and the Prophets hang on these two commandments."
—Matthew 22:37-40 NIV

I walked into my boss's office, and a sign on his wall said, "To be unclear is to be unkind." My boss wanted to talk about work, but I was totally distracted by those words. I interrupted him to ask what they meant. I could tell by his smile that he was both proud of the sign and glad I asked. He explained that not being clear can cause people to make all kinds of mistakes, and that is not fair.

Jesus's highest priorities for Christians are very clear—authentic, committed love. All His Law is based on love for Him and love for other people. We may be unclear because we are uncomfortable, unsure, or unbothered, but, in the end, it's just not kind. God is willing to have hard conversations, talk to us (and not about us), hold us accountable, and be completely honest. This could sound harsh, but these actions are examples of His kindness, another part of His character. God has made it plain that love is important to Him. You get to share His kindness by living in His clarity.

Lord,

Thank You for being clear. Loving You and loving others are not optional. Your kindness makes me want to be better. Forgive me for being unclear when I . . .

_____
_____
_____
_____
_____

The way I love people around me shows that I love You. Please give me the chance to show Your love to . . .

_____
_____
_____
_____
_____

Today, I will love You by . . .

_____
_____
_____
_____

It is well. Amen.

74

When they saw the courage of Peter and John and realized that they were unschooled, ordinary men, they were astonished and they took note that these men had been with Jesus.
—Acts 4:13 NIV

It is so funny when my sister's little dog, Tank, starts barking really loudly. I always wonder where small dogs like him get their confidence. My theory is that his big bark is completely connected to feeling secure with my sister.

In the Bible, Peter and John were confident too. They told people all about Jesus long before it was ever cool, and it got them in trouble. As Jesus's disciples, they had spent a lot of time with Him. I think this connection gave them confidence and let them speak boldly when they needed it.

Today's verse says these ordinary men defended themselves in front of a group of religious VIPs. The way they spoke blew the religious leaders' minds. Who Peter and John were (uneducated and untrained men) was not a handicap, because they were connected to a higher power, Jesus. Do you have confidence in your faith? When you talk to your friends, do they feel that confidence? Do you have the boldness to tell someone about how God has changed you? My prayer for you is that people can tell by the way you answer them that you have been with Jesus.

Lord,

Thank You for allowing me to spend time with You. Your investment in me makes me feel . . .

_____
_____
_____
_____

Who I am today should not stop me from living boldly for You. Forgive me for allowing fear to keep me from . . .

_____
_____
_____
_____

My connection to You will grow my confidence in You. Today, I will intentionally connect with You by . . .

_____
_____
_____
_____

It is well. Amen.

75

Our Lord and God, you are worthy to receive glory and honor and power, because you have created all things, and by your will they exist and were created.
—Revelation 4:11

Being accepted for who you are is the best because pretending to be someone else can be exhausting. Being able to accept yourself is even better, but that can be hard to achieve. The world says if you don't like your lips, change them. It says if your gender doesn't feel right, change it. But disliking your body is shaming it, so start learning to embrace it as a gift. A good place to begin is asking, *Am I okay being who God made me to be?*

There is a story in the Bible about a man born blind. The disciples thought he was born that way because of something he or his parents did wrong. But Jesus told them the man was blind "so that the works of God might be displayed in him" (John 9:3).

God crafted you to reflect Him. There's a real purpose and a whole plan for you. He was the architect of your life before you were even conscious, and He sees how you fit into His plan for the entire world. This means He's in charge. Are you okay with living under God's authority? God loves and accepts who you are—your lips, your gender, and all the other wonderful parts of you. He made you, and Your Father only gives good gifts.

Lord,

Thank You for making me who I am. Accepting Your plan for me makes me feel . . .

You are the boss. Forgive me for wanting to control . . .

What I trust about Your authority is . . .

Today, I ask for the courage to let You lead me to . . .

It is well. Amen.

76

This is how we have come to know love: He laid down his life for us.
—1 John 3:16

I always look forward to July, because I love watching Shark Week on the Discovery Channel! This summer I watched an episode about a family boating at a spot they go to every year. The youngest son jumped into the water and immediately saw a shark. He screamed as it swam toward him. His dad jumped into the water and punched the shark repeatedly as his son made it safely into the boat. The dad did get hurt, but he survived and said he would never regret protecting his son. This story made me think of Jesus.

Saving someone from a shark is heroic! And yet, the dad saw his actions as just doing what love does. Trust me, I will never be in *that* situation, but I have needed a dramatic rescue before. My whole life was doomed before I met Christ. And you know what? So was yours. Some of us have no idea how bad off we were before becoming a Christian; others of us have jumped right into "dangerous waters" and have an idea of what our salvation cost. Either way, the Lord Jesus paid a price. He gave His life for yours. His hands have the scars to prove He has never regretted rescuing you.

LORD,

Thank You for giving Your life to rescue mine. You pulled me out of a bad situation. Thinking about that makes me feel . . .

_____
_____
_____
_____

Your sacrifice is how I know what love is. Forgive me for not sharing Your love with . . .

_____
_____
_____
_____
_____

Today, I will show my gratitude to You by . . .

_____
_____
_____
_____

IT IS WELL. AMEN.

77

My lips will glorify you because your faithful love is better than life. So I will bless you as long as I live; at your name, I will lift up my hands. You satisfy me as with rich food; my mouth will praise you with joyful lips.
—Psalm 63:3-5

I used to have an unusual love for peanut butter. I could go through a jar in a week. A few years ago, I got really sick and lost the ability to taste. That. Was. Torture. My taste buds eventually rebounded, but things were never the same. Now I can't stand the taste of peanut butter! There were other dramatic taste changes too. I've learned to embrace this new life, and it has turned out to be a good thing in a lot of ways. My entire way of eating has been impacted, and I am making much healthier choices.

Having a relationship with God is similar. After being saved by Him, you too begin to lose your taste for some of your past habits that weren't spiritually healthy. You embrace new tastes. You make better choices as you grow in your new lifestyle, and you appreciate how change can be good. After all, the message of the gospel changed the world! It sounds like the writer of today's psalm was changed by knowing God. If you have believed in Jesus, then it has changed you for the better too. God always knows how to satisfy those who are truly His.

Lord,

Thank You for the message of the gospel. As long as I live, I will bless You for . . .

_____
_____
_____
_____
_____

I want to be satisfied in You. Forgive me for going back to my old ways to find . . .

_____
_____
_____
_____
_____
_____
_____

This new life in You means new taste buds and new choices. Today I choose . . .

_____
_____
_____
_____
_____
_____

It is well. Amen.

78

Every wise woman builds her house, but a foolish one tears it down with her own hands.
—Proverbs 14:1

Both of my grandmothers had recipes that were my favorite. Grandma E made the silkiest sweet potato pie, and Grandma C made the greatest mac and cheese. In my kitchen, I have their rolling pin and stirring spoon to remind me of the greatness they created in their kitchens and the impression they made on my heart. They shared food, wisdom, and fun and provided me a sense of comfort in ways only grandmothers can. My friends call these gems "girl magic," and they are gathered by being a daughter, a sister, a mom, a woman, a girl.

God celebrates our femaleness, and He wants us to love the unique gifts that come with it. We see His design in Rebekah's hospitality, Anna's hope, Ruth's loyalty, Abigail's bravery, Priscilla's leadership, Hannah's faith, Jochebed's planning, Mary's wisdom, and the uniqueness of you. If you are wise, you will learn what it means to build beauty, faith, hope, balance, peace, passion, and connection because there really is something beautiful found in the "girlness" of being a girl.

Lord,

Thank You for making me female. It is a gift You were intentional to give. You didn't make me by mistake. Forgive me for doubting Your plan for . . .

You celebrate women. Please teach me to love and celebrate how You made me to . . .

I want to be a wise woman. Today I will start by . . .

It is well. Amen.

79

The one who does not love does not know God, because God is love.
—1 John 4:8

As Christians, we believe that God created everything, so every good thing we enjoy is a gift from Him. We literally owe it all to Him. One of the most beautiful things He has shared with us is love. Today's verse makes it clear that God *is* love. He both creates and shows love because it comes from who He is.

People try to redefine love without God. When they do, they miss so much of the beauty that's part of His creation. This matters because you are a product of His love. Your identity, future, and life in Christ all exist because of His love for you. A verse in 1 Corinthians 13 shares what it is like to experience God's perfect love. His love is patient, kind, not jealous, not rude. It hopes all things and endures all things. This is more than a description of Him; it's a picture of your life in a relationship with Him. God is love. And that love is more than a feeling; it's a beautiful experience.

Lord,

Thank You for giving Yourself to me. Love is who You are, and that is a gift to me. Forgive me for questioning that when . . .

_____
_____
_____
_____
_____

You have created beauty, and that includes me. Knowing this makes me feel . . .

_____
_____
_____
_____
_____

Who I am is because of Your love. So today I will share Your love by . . .

_____
_____
_____
_____
_____

It is well. Amen.

80

God, create a clean heart for me and renew a steadfast spirit within me.
—Psalm 51:10

Two of my best friends and I became an a cappella group in high school. We sang at our church and community events and whenever and wherever one of my uncles asked us to. (Three of my uncles were pastors.) Singing gave me my first glimpse of the truth of God's Word. Learning lyrics pulled straight from the Bible helped grow me spiritually. We sang a song called "Give Me a Clean Heart"—its lyrics come from today's verse—and it was my favorite. I still sing it to remind myself how much I need the Lord.

The prayer in Psalm 51 is a humble one. David is not asking God to change his situation; he is asking God to change him. He knew God saw what was going on inside his heart, and David was willing to be real about the mess his had been.

The Bible says your heart is the center of who you are. The heart is mentioned over a thousand times in the Bible—it's a really big deal. As a Christian you have been made new, but your heart still wrestles with its past. As soon as you are real about the condition of your heart, David's prayer can become your prayer too.

Lord,

Thank You for knowing me so well. Your love for me makes me safe. You know I still struggle with sin. Please forgive me for...

I do want a clean heart. This means I need to be honest about...

Today I am asking humbly for You to help me...

It is well. Amen.

LORD, here's who and what I'm praying for . . .

I'm grateful You've answered these prayers . . .

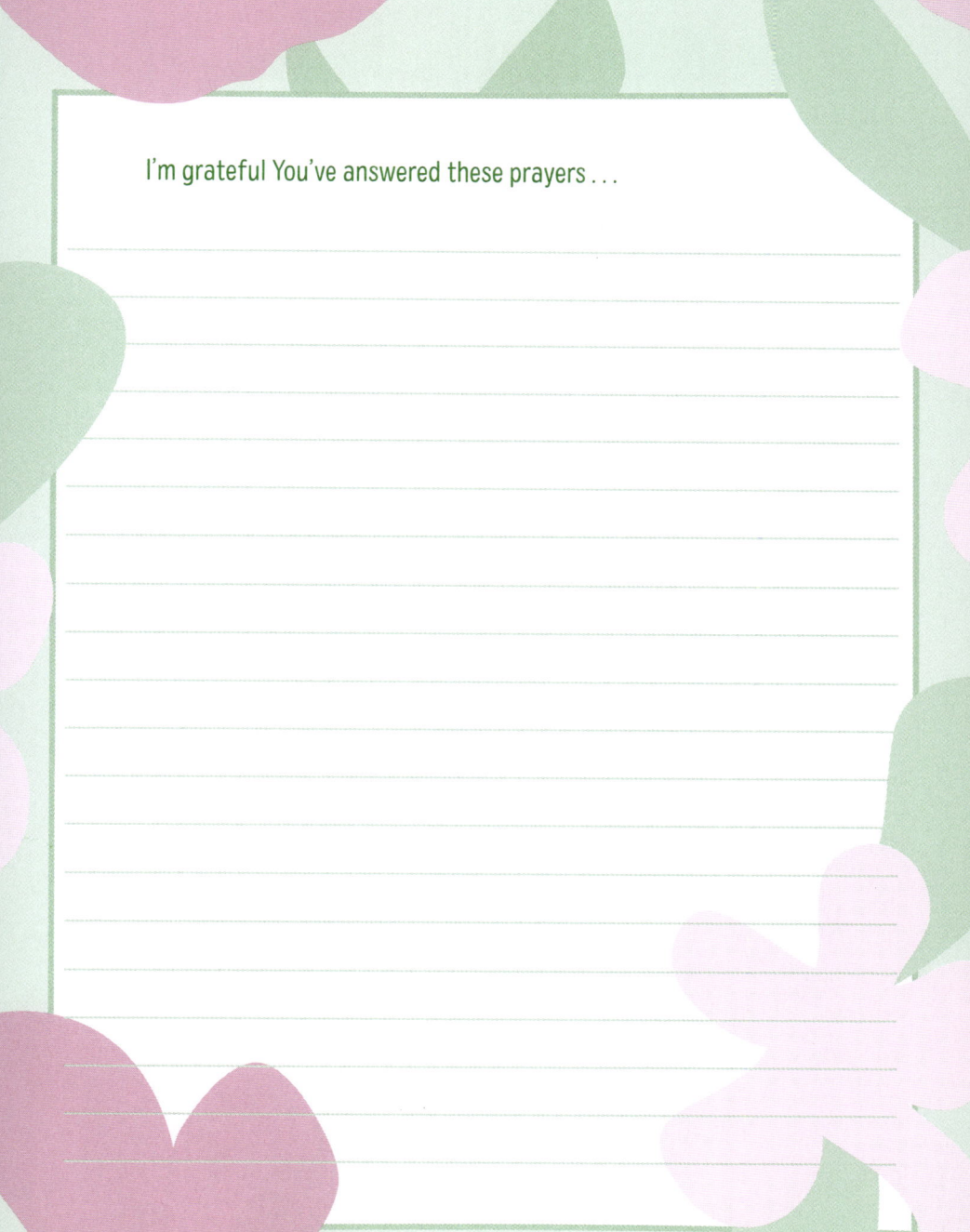

81

We are afflicted in every way but not crushed; we are perplexed but not in despair; we are persecuted but not abandoned; we are struck down but not destroyed.
—2 Corinthians 4:8-9

Even though I was committed to good grades, school was always overwhelming. The rest of my life didn't stop because I had homework or a project due the next day. Sometimes track practice, choir practice, and being the oldest sibling made doing schoolwork feel like true suffering. To get through the work and all the other, harder things, I rehearsed and recited Paul's words in 2 Corinthians 4:8-9.

In these verses Paul is talking about suffering. You might be asking, "But why?" Some dramatic things are going on in these verses, and I totally understand if you are a little concerned. Paul had experience with suffering. He understood that when we're upset, we don't always think clearly. He wants you to know that suffering is not a punishment. That is important. The world is broken by sin, and suffering is a consequence. But trust me (and Paul), God is able to remix the hard times and use them to make your faith stronger. Strong faith helps you get through the "schoolwork" that your life is sure to bring.

Lord,

Thank You for not letting my suffering be a waste of time. You use everything in my life to make me more like Jesus. This makes me feel . . .

Suffering is a part of everyone's life. Please forgive me for thinking . . .

When I look back, I can see that You have been teaching me . . .

I want You to grow my faith. Starting today, when things are harc, I will . . .

It is well. Amen.

82

"This way you will remember and obey all my commands and be holy to your God."
—Numbers 15:40

I watched a movie about a guy with a condition that kept him from being able to create new memories. He carried photos of people and surroundings with notes written on them to get through his days safely. Without memories, he had to constantly look through the photos and read the notes to see if he knew the person he was talking to. He could never be sure what was true.

Today's verse comes from a conversation between the Lord and His people, the Israelites, through Moses. God was making sure their hearts were committed to Him. The best way for them, and you, to stay committed to God is to remember all that God has done. Remembering His acts allows you to be sure of what is true about God, rather than having to constantly figure out what is real about what's in front of you. When you know what is true, you can live out your faith, being happy to obey God because He has a track record of being good and true.

Lord,

Thank You for being good to me. Whenever I am unsure, I have Your goodness to look back on. What this teaches me about You is . . .

_____
_____
_____
_____

Remembering Your truth helps me obey You. Please forgive me for forgetting . . .

_____
_____
_____
_____

You have shown Your goodness to me by . . .

_____
_____
_____
_____

I want to be obedient to You. If my heart starts to wander away from You, I will remember . . .

_____
_____
_____

It is well. Amen.

83

In the same way we who are many are one body in Christ and individually members of one another.
—Romans 12:5

Growing up, my family and the people in my neighborhood were all pretty close. Everybody took care of everybody else. This community made me feel connected and responsible. The new, bigger family I gained through my church gave me relationships that made me feel valuable. When we become Christians, our new lives fill with new hope, new expectations, new purpose, and new relationships. Your church's job is to surround you, support you, and send you out to be who God has made you to be.

Jesus showed us what community could look like when He took twelve men, turned them into a family, taught them about Him, gave them new work to do, and sent them out to do it. Jesus has included you in His community, too, which is a big encouragement. You have a new, unique purpose. God has a mission for you. The church is a gift to you, and you and your mission are a gift to the church. Together, you and your church can let the world see God's beauty.

Lord,

Thank You for giving me a new family. You have welcomed me into Your community. This makes me feel . . .

_____
_____
_____
_____
_____

You have important work for me to do. Forgive me for when I only want . . .

_____
_____
_____
_____
_____

As a part of Your church, I want to support other Christians. Today, I pray for the chance to . . .

_____
_____
_____
_____
_____

It is well. Amen.

84

For I want very much to see you, so that I may impart to you some spiritual gift to strengthen you, that is, to be mutually encouraged by each other's faith, both yours and mine.
—Romans 1:11-12

We use family language when we become Christians. Knowing God gives us access to relationship with Him and His family. The church is where we learn how to know God. This takes time, but it can be helped along by people investing in you and teaching you. We call this "discipleship." Although I didn't understand the full value of discipleship when I was younger, being part of a church who loved Jesus made up for the things my family couldn't provide. It was valuable discipleship.

Discipleship is a relationship that helps people grow in their Christian faith. I am always looking for the opportunity to experience it. I want to be taught, challenged, reoriented, and supported. If you don't have a more mature Christian investing in you, you need one. Pray and ask the Lord to send someone. Don't be afraid to ask. Discipleship helps provide access to a deeper relationship with God, and this access can change lives. Remember that a seed (that's you) is a potential tree, but it has to go through a process. It needs help from the soil, roots, air, and water to grow into what it is meant to be.

Lord,

Thank You for giving me access to You. To know You more is to be a better me. My access to You has already made me . . .

_____
_____
_____
_____

A discipleship relationship is an investment in spiritual growth. Forgive me for not growing when I'm investing in . . .

_____
_____
_____
_____

Being around people who love You is impactful for me. Please allow me to share that same love for You with . . .

_____
_____
_____
_____
_____

It is well. Amen.

85

But the fruit of the Spirit is love, joy, peace, patience, kindness, goodness, faithfulness, gentleness, and self-control.
—Galatians 5:22-23

We were moving again. This time we were moving back to the city into a row home on the corner with a little yard and a big red deck off the second floor in the back. It was summer and too hot to be moving! My friend noticed the one big tree in the little yard—it had large, beautiful, ripe, sweet peaches growing on it. Everything stopped as we sat on the deck being refreshed by peaches. Who knew peach trees grew in the middle of the city?

Not too long after that, it struck me that a peach tree doesn't really benefit from the fruit it produces. It grows the peaches, and we eat them. As Christians, we grow fruit too. Today's verse lists the kind of fruit Jesus talked about during His time on earth. It's interesting that, like the peach tree, the fruit we grow usually benefits the people around us. This doesn't mean the fruit is not helpful for us too, but every tree that grows well produces more than enough fruit to share.

Lord,

Thank You for the benefits of growing spiritual fruit. It all helps me to be more like You. One fruit of the Spirit I want to grow more of is . . .

The fruit in my life is supposed to be good for others. Please forgive me for when I may have avoided . . .

I am praying for the opportunity to bless someone else by . . .

It is well. Amen.

86

"I am the good shepherd. I know my own, and my own know me."
—John 10:14

I have gone to lots of different schools. One of my favorites was a school for the deaf. This school sparked my passion for American Sign Language (ASL). I took classes, taught myself, and practiced by signing songs in church. To this day I love to watch ASL interpreters at conferences, at concerts, and on the news.

One day during a weather emergency, I watched the interpreter and realized right away that she was not using sign language at all. She was a complete imposter! Clearly, knowing sign language is not the same as knowing about it. The interpreter may have fooled the people in the room, but actual signers can easily tell the difference.

The same is true of your faith. Knowing Jesus is not the same as knowing about Jesus. Hanging out with Christians is great, but it is different from loving Christ yourself. Authentic Jesus lovers can eventually catch the poser. Much like how the fake signer put deaf people in that community in danger, not knowing Jesus has consequences too.

Lord,

Thank You for allowing me to really know You. You want a relationship with me! The idea of that makes me feel . . .

_____
_____
_____
_____

One of the great things about knowing You is . . .

_____
_____
_____
_____

Knowing You is so good for me. Please forgive me for when I skip time with You to . . .

_____
_____
_____
_____

Today I want to invest in our relationship by . . .

_____
_____
_____

It is well. Amen.

87

Charm is deceptive and beauty is fleeting, but a woman who fears the Lord will be praised.
—Proverbs 31:30

I have sisters, and we don't look alike at all. Because of their hair, skin color, and other features, I convinced myself I was the "less cute" sister. This thinking led me to believe I was less valuable. That then spiraled into the idea that cute girls are more loved and wanted. It's amazing—and troubling—how easy it was to believe all that. As I got older, I learned that being beautiful on the outside does not make someone beautiful on the inside. For me, that's when who I am inside became way more important.

We all know that internal beauty trumps external beauty, but the world we live in screams that the outside is what's important. Thoughts about how your body looks are called "body image," and it has probably been on your mind for years already. Diets, makeup, clothes, jewelry—these are not bad things. But they don't make you pretty. Believing the truth about your cuteness starts with believing the truth about God being good. To know your worth, you need to know God's heart.

Lord,

Thank You that the basis of true beauty is who You made me to be inside. Sometimes I need to be reminded of that. Honestly, I have wanted You to change my . . .

You gave me the hair, skin, eyes, and lips that You wanted me to have. Forgive me for not appreciating my . . .

My inner beauty tells who I am. Please help me to become more . . .

It is well. Amen.

88

And if someone overpowers one person, two can resist him. A cord of three strands is not easily broken.
—Ecclesiastes 4:12

Do you watch shows on National Geographic? My family loves that stuff. Our favorite shows to watch are about predators and prey. The hunting animals are usually very strategic. They watch a group to find the weakest one. When the predator pounces, and the prey scatters, the hunter already knows what direction to run in: the same direction as the weakest member of the group. Once the hunter isolates the weakest one, the outcome becomes unavoidable. Smart, right? Everyone in our house huddles around any sized screen to watch it happen. All of us except Eden, who boycotts watching anything getting hurt.

The things that make *your* family unique may be exactly what turns you off. Being vegans, a blended family, or even Christians can make you want to pull away to be alone. It's okay to have preferences; we all do. But God created you to thrive with people. The enemy's goal is to pull you away so that he can pick you off like prey. You can't always exchange your friends and family, but you can remember that God can use them. You are always more vulnerable if you are immature, weak, or constantly alone. Sticking with the right group is always wise. Today's verse teaches us there is safety in numbers.

Lord,

Thank You for giving me other people. Help me to see them as a gift from You. You use safe people to provide protection. Thank You for . . .

Relationships can be hard. Forgive me for when I make it harder by . . .

It is not good to be isolated. Today, help me to be a good friend by . . .

It is well. Amen.

89

He responded, "Not everyone can accept this saying, but only those to whom it has been given."
—Matthew 19:11

Sometimes accepting things that happen in life can me feel weak, like I don't have real choices. But growing from these things is a choice, and that's not weak. Thankfully, not all acceptance is bad. The best thing I ever accepted was the Lord's gift of salvation. If you are a Christian, then the same is true for you.

Think about some other things to accept about your faith. You can accept that when you're a mess, God can get His greatest glory from your life. You can accept that even though you're unable to control what anyone else believes, you're still able to pray, encourage, share, and trust the Holy Spirit. You can accept that you can never know somebody else's heart, but you can make your faith look attractive to your friends. You can accept that you won't be protected from all hurt or danger but that the Lord has promised to be with you. Most importantly, you can accept and expect that your faith will change you.

Lord,

Thank You for allowing me to accept Your truth. Your wisdom helps me grow. What I learned about myself today is . . .

_____

I want to accept You are in control. Forgive me for not accepting . . .

_____

Letting You lead is always safe. Today, I am glad to accept . . .

_____

It is well. Amen.

90

But you, dear friends, remember what was predicted by the apostles of our Lord Jesus Christ. They told you, "In the end time there will be scoffers living according to their own ungodly desires." These people create divisions and are worldly, not having the Spirit.
—Jude 1:17–19

I did a study on the book of Jude. It is a letter written to warn the members of a church that the bad behaviors going on outside the church were beginning to show up inside it. Jude understood that people who didn't follow Jesus would be selfish, mean, petty, disloyal—the list can go on. The sad part was Jude heard that followers of Jesus were acting in those ways too. They were starting to look less and less like Jesus.

What does this study of Jude have to do with you? The same thing can happen in your church. And every church member is responsible for changing it, including you. The way you help is by knowing what you believe. You've been taught about the role of women, the value of life, and how to spend your money. Your beliefs impact how you live as a Christian, as a girl, and as a member of your church. You help by praying for your church, confessing your bad behaviors, and forgiving people for theirs. You help your church by working on your own healing and then helping others to heal. Remember, your faithfulness can be used to impact your entire church!

Lord,

Thank You for my part in helping my church. My age is not important; my belief in You is. This makes me feel . . .

The church is important to You. Forgive me when I have treated it like . . .

My life as a Christian is impactful. I want to help my church by . . .

It is well. Amen.

LORD, here's who and what I'm praying for . . .

I'm grateful You've answered these prayers . . .

91

If we walk in the light as he himself is in the light, we have fellowship with one another, and the blood of Jesus his Son cleanses us from all sin.
—1 John 1:7

Everybody has secrets. Your family has secrets, your friends have secrets, and it's no secret that you do too. Secrets can be fun when you are planning a surprise party or making someone's day with an unplanned visit. Secrets can be safe when it's the combination to your bike lock or the password to your bank account. But secrets are dangerous when you hide habits that are unhealthy or when you cover them with lies. Living in secrecy like that is called darkness. The remedy is God's light.

Satan wants you to believe lies about your sin. He wants you to think that what you watch or listen to is not a big deal. He wants you to find ways to justify your bad decisions so that you will keep making them. Satan wants you to discount the effects that your sin has on you. But sin will always disrupt relationships, including your relationship with God. And excusing your own sin doesn't work; forgiveness is up to God only. Finally, Satan wants you to keep your sins hidden. Left unchecked, sins often start small and become bigger and bigger. But darkness is never the answer. God tells us to walk in the light.

Lord,

Thank You for shining light into the dark places of my life. Darkness does not give me life. I am learning that You . . .

Secrets can be dangerous. Forgive me for trying to hide . . .

I choose to walk in the light. Today I confess . . .

I'm grateful for Your forgiveness.

It is well. Amen.

92

Be devoted to one another in love. Honor one another above yourselves. Never be lacking in zeal, but keep your spiritual fervor, serving the Lord. Be joyful in hope, patient in affliction, faithful in prayer. Share with the Lord's people who are in need. Practice hospitality.
—Romans 12:10-13 NIV

My friend Krystal has a sign in her house that says, "Be strong enough to stand alone. Smart enough to know when you need help. And brave enough to ask for it." Every time I read that sign, it sounds so wise but also so hard to do. I personally feel great about standing alone. But then it all starts to fall apart. According to what the sign says, I probably need to learn to ask for help. One day I sat through a session that was supposed to help me understand my personality, and one of the biggest lessons I learned is that I need friends. Good thing I have Krystal!

These verses in Romans are a good description of what it takes to build a strong friendship. It doesn't just happen; it takes effort. Friendships are not one-sided and all about you. They aren't overly demanding, jealous, or shallow. Being humble is a must because true friends honor each other above themselves. True friends make you better and are glad to help when you need it. Friendships are a big part of your identity—your friends tell a lot about you. So be sure your friendships are fed with love, devotion, and prayer.

LORD,

Thank You for making friendship. Good ones make me so much better. Thinking about Your gift of friendship makes me feel . . .

Friendships take work. Forgive me for when I'm slacking by . . .

I want to be a good friend. Today I will do that by . . .

IT IS WELL. AMEN.

93

And my God will supply all your needs according to his riches in glory in Christ Jesus.
—Philippians 4:19

A wall in my living room has my favorite sayings on it. The shortest one has the biggest truth: "Christ is enough." It sounds so simple, but those three words mean so much for our lives. The idea that God is enough is what Satan lied to Eve about. Eve fell for the lie. If I am honest, sometimes I do too. I trick myself into thinking I would be happy if I had more money, a better car, or a different house. I bet you deal with this too. You may be thinking, *If only I had better grades, cooler clothes, the attention of boys, more popularity, more freedom . . .*

It takes faith to believe that God + Zero = Everything. Clothes, vacations, and pets are all good to have. Friendships are great to have too; the Bible says so. The problem isn't always that we want more; it's usually that we don't want Christ. This happens when we don't believe that He is enough. Let me encourage you to remember today's verse. God will take care of what we need.

Lord,

Thank You for being everything I need. My friends and my things make it hard to see that sometimes. To trust that You are enough feels . . .

Forgive me for when I trust myself for . . .

You are everything I need. I want to stop relying on . . .

It is well. Amen.

94

May the God of hope fill you with all joy and peace in believing, so that by the power of the Holy Spirit you may abound in hope.
—Romans 15:13 ESV

Right next to the mirror in the bathroom I have a sign that says, "Don't believe everything you think." When one of my daughters was in crisis, wrestling with her faith, I would remind her of it. My hope was that she would identify the lies she had been believing and then do the work to address them.

The enemy uses our wounds and our pride to create chaos in our lives. This chaos keeps us from recognizing his lies and distracts us from dealing with root issues that need to be faced.

Identity is not just what we look like. So much of it is what we believe. This is why it's important that you recognize Satan's lies and address the sin issues in your life. So do it. Deal with your fears: the fear of ruining that relationship, failing that test, or feeling inadequate. Address the reasons for your sadness, your anger, your indifference. You need to remove the chaos and focus on the God of hope. In Romans 15, Paul prays that God would fill you with all joy and peace in believing. These are two necessary tools to make sure you don't believe everything you think.

Lord,

Thank You for challenging me to address my issues. Just like Paul, You want me filled with joy, peace, belief, and hope. The idea of dealing with issues in my life feels like . . .

You don't want me to believe the enemy's lies. Forgive me for when I do believe them instead of believing . . .

Today, I have Your peace, so I will focus on . . .

It is well. Amen.

95

Carry one another's burdens; in this way you will fulfill the law of Christ.
—Galatians 6:2

The last thing I want to be known as is needy. As a big sister, I like being the one taking care of things. In a book called *Side by Side*, Dr. Edward Welch says God made us with a basic need to be in a community. This is a Christian truth that I say I accept, but most days I don't want to. Avoiding my need for help means the broken parts of my life keep me vulnerable and weak. I read something else interesting in the book: we have both a neediness and a "neededness," and they each create value in our lives. Now that's a plot twist!

Our lives have so much going on. Whether or not we like it, we need help from the Lord and our friends and family. We need to hear that we're wrong, to be encouraged, and to be challenged to be better. But we are also *needed*. The Holy Spirit uses us to build intentional relationships where we pray, help, and encourage each other. We learn to be the kind of friends who help people become more like Jesus.

You need community. But part of your Christian journey is also meeting the needs of others.

Lord,

Thank You for the Holy Spirit's help. He helps me grow good fruit. You made me to thrive in community. Forgive me for when I don't because . . .

When I think about being needy, I feel . . .

When I think about being needed, I feel . . .

To build my community, today I will . . .

It is well. Amen.

96

Sanctify them by the truth; your word is truth.
—John 17:17

Do you recognize the name Suzanne Collins? She is the author of The Hunger Games series. It has sold over 100 million copies and has been translated into fifty-five languages. That is impressive! What's interesting is that she wrote a four-part series that has been made into three movies, and we haven't learned one important thing about her through them. You know why? Because the books are fiction, written to entertain. So it's okay for Suzanne to stay distant and unknown to you. Who she is doesn't change who you are.

You know who God is, right? Have you read His series? It's one book made up of a collection of sixty-six books translated into over six hundred languages. One of the key differences between the Bible and *The Hunger Games* is that the Bible is not fiction. And the author, God, wants you to know the truth (not your truth or my truth but the actual truth) about who He is. God may be invisible, but He is not fictional, and neither are His words! The Bible is God's gift to us. In it is a plan for your salvation that changes everything because of who He is.

Lord,

Thank You for giving me the Bible as Your truth. It is real and impacts everything. Christians should love Your words. Forgive me taking those words for granted by . . .

The Bible is important for me because . . .

The Bible is where I learn about You. Today I commit to read . . .

It is well. Amen.

97

*But he said to me, "My grace is sufficient for you,
for my power is perfected in weakness."*
—2 Corinthians 12:9

I am one of those few people who have had the chicken pox twice. Many people today have never had it, but I managed to hit the jackpot. Both times were awful, but the first time was better because my cousins and I had it together. We got to stay home from school for a week at Grandma's, and it was almost fun. But the second time around, I had it alone. I felt so sick and lonely and sad. The illness was the same, and the suffering was unavoidable, but the way I responded was all up to me.

A royal queen on a show I watched said, "Suffering is as cheap as dirt... What matters is what you make of it." What she was talking about was fictional, but what she was saying was factual. Everyone suffers. If you haven't already, you will. The way that you get through these hard seasons will be impacted by how you respond to them. It matters how you handle your suffering. In your pain you can learn more about the Lord and yourself. The situation may not be any easier, but you'll know God can use it. And in your weakness, you will see His power in its perfection.

Lord,

Thank You for Your grace and power. Your work in me is always good. It matters how I respond to my suffering. Forgive me for not seeing the way You . . .

When things are hard, I usually react by . . .

I want to learn to respond to suffering by . . .

It is well. Amen.

98

At that time you were without Christ, excluded from the citizenship of Israel, and foreigners to the covenants of promise, without hope and without God in the world. But now in Christ Jesus, you who were far away have been brought near by the blood of Christ.
—Ephesians 2:12–13

I've had identity issues since I was little. It started in Germany when I was the only black girl in school. I was accepted but still different. When we moved to the U.S., my skin color became an issue, and I also liked German foods and used German words. I just felt different than everyone else.

But at our church, I met people with all kinds of life experiences. They welcomed me home, and I began to feel "normal" again. Until then, I *felt* foreign, but God used His people to give me a connection. I *was* far away, and He brought me near.

That early part of my story used to embarrass me. But it's important for me to look back and remember how God used His church to show His kindness. As God's daughter, you can look back at the hope He's given you. You have been brought near too. The promises He's kept should inspire you to share Him with others. God wants to take your experiences and use them to impact your community. Using your individual journey and mine, He weaves a tapestry that links Christians together in His big church.

God can use you! As you enjoy His gifts, you get to show off the Giver.

Lord,

Thank You for rescuing me. You have brought me near to You. That reality makes me feel . . .

_____
_____
_____
_____

My journey is important to You. Forgive me for forgetting that You . . .

_____
_____
_____
_____

What I am learning about myself is . . .

_____
_____
_____
_____

I want to be used by You in my community. But I have to remember to stay grateful for . . .

_____
_____
_____
_____

It is well. Amen.

99

Very early in the morning, while it was still dark, he got up, went out, and made his way to a deserted place; and there he was praying.
—Mark 1:35

My fifth-grade teacher was Mr. McKinney. I had his wife in fourth grade, and she told him that I was a good student but talked too much. When it started happening in his class, he moved me to the back of the room away from everyone else, gave me books to read, and made me write reports. I hated the extra work but loved the attention. It inspired a passion for reading that has stayed with me. I also earned a life lesson: sometimes it takes being removed from the distractions to focus on the work that can change my life.

Being connected can be such a good thing. Having access to people and resources whenever you need them is a game changer. But being disconnected can be a good thing too. Jesus did it and clearly did not struggle with FOMO. He modeled getting away like it was His life support. Probably because it was. Jesus removed Himself to talk to the Father, to be led by the Spirit, to think, strategize, and rest. Whenever He returned, He did the things He was supposed to do, like starting His public ministry. If you followed Jesus's lead and removed yourself from distractions, imagine how your life could be impacted.

Lord,

Thank You for being my role model. Just saying that makes me feel . . .

Stopping to be with You is important. Forgive me for not prioritizing . . .

Having distraction-free moments allows me to . . .

Lord, please teach me how to get away so I can . . .

It is well. Amen.

100

Then the Lord said to Moses, "Tell Aaron and his sons to bless the people of Israel with this special blessing: 'May the Lord bless you and protect you. May the Lord smile on you and be gracious to you. May the Lord show you his favor and give you his peace.'"
—Numbers 6:22-26 NLT

My mom is a prayer warrior. Whenever I have something going on, I call her because she prays like she is literally standing in front of God's throne. I'm blessed to have watched her pray all of my life. Her example made me believe in prayer too. I am so convinced that God hears me that I'll pray about anything in my life. But I usually pray about me. One day I read that prayer is a gift that you can give to the people you love. Makes sense—it's free, won't get lost in the mail, and doesn't have to be wrapped (#winning)!

Praying for others takes the focus off you. It's a habit that reminds you God is working in other people's lives and that you care. Today's prayer from the book of Numbers comes directly from the Lord. God told Aaron to pray it over the people in Israel so that they would be blessed. Prayer is your opportunity to ask God to bless others too. If it worked for Aaron and Moses, you can trust that God will make it work for you. Prayer is the very best gift you can give.

Lord,

Thank You for teaching me more about prayer. It's my chance to share my life with You. What these verses teach me about You is...

You want me to pray for my friends. Forgive me for when I forget that and...

I want to be in the habit of praying for others. Today, I ask You to bless...

It is well. Amen.

LORD, here's who and what I'm praying for . . .

I'm grateful You've answered these prayers . . .

You may have finished this journal but not your journey! Don't stop praying; you get to enjoy a lifetime with Jesus. If you are not a Christian, it is not too late. Talk to the Lord (you know He enjoys it), confess your sins to Him, and acknowledge your need for Him. He loves you and has been waiting patiently. My prayer for you now is this:

> *I pray that you, being
> rooted and firmly established in love,
> may be able to comprehend with all the saints
> what is the length and width, height and depth
> of God's love, and to know Christ's love that
> surpasses knowledge, so that you may be
> filled with all the fullness of God.*
> —Ephesians 3:17-19

Page 114. John Maxwell, *Be a People Person: Effective Leadership Through Effective Relationships* (Colorado Springs, CO: David C. Cook, 2007), 26.
Page 130. David Platt, *Radical: Taking Back Your Faith from the American Dream* (Colorado Springs, CO: Multnomah, 2010), 7.